LOVE LETTERS FROM THE HEART OF TEXAS

*Sermons from St. Paul's
Episcopal Church – Brady*

BRADY
THE TRUE HEART OF
TEXAS

Second Edition

Published by

ARCHDEACON BOOKS

Hoover, Alabama

Hardback ISBN: 978-1-949422-87-0
Paperback ISBN: 978-1-949422-88-7
Kindle ISBN: 978-1-949422-98-6

Editor's Note to the Reader

The sequencing – or the order of these sermons – follows the Liturgical Year Lectionary in the *1979 Book of Common Prayer*.

The first day of the Church calendar year is the First Sunday of Advent, which sometimes occurs on the last Sunday in November but mostly on the first Sunday in December.

The meditations, reflections, and sermons selected for this book begin with Ash Wednesday 2024 (the first day in the Liturgical Season of Lent) which is well into the Liturgical Year B. There are three years (A, B, and C) in which much of the Bible is read during the service of Holy Communion.

December 1, 2024, was the First Sunday of Advent; however, the sermon for that day is not included in this edition.

The standard of the Lectionary includes a Psalm; selected readings from the Old Testament, the New Testament; and one of the four Gospel versions. Traditionally, the priest (preacher) delivers his sermon according to one of the selected Lectionary readings, normally the Gospel – but the priest may decide otherwise.

ASH WEDNESDAY

February 14, 2024

This past Sunday, I made a brief reference in my sermon to the Super Bowl, specifically the Super Bowl commercials, and how corporations would spend something like seven million dollars to try and capture our attention in about 30 seconds... all for their benefit.

Well, guess what? One of the first commercials to be shown caused me to stop what I was doing and pay attention... for my benefit. I haven't Googled the internet to see what kind of reaction it garnered. Nor have I watched the commercial repeatedly. I went to YouTube to view it once to ensure my first impression was somewhat accurate.

I found this commercial to be both profound and provocative.

The commercial portrayed, in still form, different scenarios of American life. Some of the pseudo paintings, we could call them, represented a so-called privileged individual of our society washing the feet of one deemed outcast by our society. Maybe four or five such images were sent into our living room in a very short time.

After the final image, a single sentence appeared above a dark background. The message was this:

Jesus did not teach hate. He washed feet.

Just as Valentine's Day coincides with Ash Wednesday, Super Bowl Sunday catapulted us to Maundy Thursday.

Not everybody in our culture knows the story of Maundy Thursday. But we do. On the night before Jesus went to the cross to die for the sins of humanity, Jesus washed the feet of his disciples. Jesus served his closest followers in their vulnerable state, and Jesus called them to follow his example. The call was not only for Jesus' first disciples; Jesus issues the same call to us to serve the most vulnerable in his name.

This is the mandate of Jesus (that is where the word Maundy comes from). This is the mandate of Jesus, to love one another as Jesus loves us, especially those whom society wrongly deems to be unworthy of love, both God's love and our love.

Yet when we deem a person or a group unworthy of love, we give ourselves permission to hate, which goes against the message of that Super Bowl commercial.

It goes against the Gospel of Jesus Christ, so it is front and center in the Collect of the Day for Ash Wednesday, which the Church has prayed for ages. It begins:

Almighty and everlasting God, you hate nothing you have made and forgive the sins of all who are penitent...
(1979 BCP page 264)
God hates nothing that God has made.

We need to let that sink in.

God hates nothing that God has made.

Well, if God hates nothing that God has made, what gives me the right to hate anything, anyone, whom God has made?

What gives me the right to exclude certain people from the church?

What gives me the right to marginalize people in our larger community?

As I have reflected on my own capacity to hate... which is far greater than I prefer, what I notice about myself is I am tempted to hate those who I at first believe are to me a threat, credible or not. My hate is rooted in my fear.

Now, I will grant you that a certain amount of fear is healthy. Evil exists in this world. God did not make evil; evil is the result of human sin. Therefore, evil exists. So, we need to be on the alert.

I am not the kind of parent who allowed my children to play in the street when they were younger or walk around the house with knives. During the interview process here, I was relieved that St. Paul's locks the doors of its sanctuary at night. That was a genuine concern for me and my family, and a comfort to know that you see reality for what it is.

So, yes, a reasonable amount of fear is necessary.

What I am talking about is irrational fear, the type of anxiety that comes without critical thinking, the anxiety that drives me to place a label on an individual or group, a label that causes me to determine that such an individual group is outside the scope of God's love. And if such people, according to my judgment, are outside the scope of God's love, then I can hate them to the best of my ability, to the glory of God.

Well, this sinful line of thinking has its roots in a zero-sum game. After all, everything else in our life is zero-sum. For me to win, you have to lose. For the Chiefs to continually win the Super Bowl, 31 other teams (including the Cowboys) must always lose. If I want something, you cannot have it. This is the air we breathe.

And we wrongly apply this flawed logic to our relationship with God. For God to love me, God cannot possibly love you. God must hate you, so let me come up with the reasons why God must hate you.

Except, God hates nothing that God has made.

And fortunately, that is not all. Not only does God hate nothing that God has made, but God stands ready to forgive me for thinking that God has to hate someone else to love me, and to transform my heart and actions through God's Holy Spirit, so that I not only acknowledge the many ways I have wrongly hated others in the past but to become merciful to others in the same way that God is merciful to me.

***

In a moment, we will pray the Litany of Penitence. These historic, thoughtful, well-crafted, profound, provocative, and holy petitions will call to mind where we fall short in this life, where we give ourselves over to hate in its various forms. This will be a common theme as we make our way through the penitential season of Lent.

If we take tonight's liturgy to heart, if we genuinely embrace our Lenten journey, we will come face-to-face with the worst of ourselves.

But I cannot allow my identification as a "wretched, miserable offender with manifold sins and wickedness" to be the goal of Lent nor can I allow my natural aversion to acknowledging my worst self to become an excuse to skip Lent, to ignore the horrors of Good Friday, to get as quickly as I can to the joys of Easter Sunday.

Before we can truly embrace the Good News of the God who became human in the person of Jesus of Nazareth, we must be realistic about the bad news.

We are sinners.

We are mortal, fallen creatures.

We have an almost unlimited capacity to hate those who differ from us and act on that hate in ways both small and big which, ironically, sometimes makes us want to hate ourselves. And the day is coming when we will be called before God to give an account on how we lived our lives.

But please hear this.

When we see ourselves for who we are in our most vulnerable state, Jesus comes to us, serves us, and empowers us to claim the truth that we are created in the image of God, and our mission then becomes to grow into the likeness of the God revealed in Jesus.

This Lent, choose to grow into the likeness of Jesus.

Work toward becoming the person God is creating you to be.

You can know that God loves you in Jesus and you can trust that God could never hate you. Therefore, you should not hate yourself. You are loved, which means you have an infinite capacity to love, to love yourself and others.

From the Book of Common Prayer:
Almighty and everlasting God, you hate nothing you have made and forgive the sins of all who are penitent: Create and make in us new and contrite hearts, that we, worthily lamenting our sins and acknowledging our wretchedness, may obtain of you, the God of all mercy, perfect remission and forgiveness; through Jesus Christ our Lord, who lives and reigns with you and the Holy Spirit, one God, for ever and ever. Amen.

PALM SUNDAY

March 24, 2024

I have a growing list of questions I plan to ask God when I die and enter God's direct presence Not that I am in any hurry to do this. Some of those questions are rooted in passages of Scripture where I hunger for more detail. One of those passages appears in this morning's Passion narrative. It is a piece of detail which, if we allow it to, gives us pause.

It is a moment when Pontius Pilate, the Roman governor of Judea roughly two thousand years ago, is trying to keep the peace in an anxious time. It is the week of the Jewish Passover, the time when Jewish people remember how God liberated them from the bondage of Pharaoh in Egypt. Jewish people most certainly drew parallels to the Roman occupation of their homeland in Jesus' time to slavery under Pharaoh.

It was customary then for the Roman government to release a Jewish prisoner for the Passover, a sort of pardon.

Pontius Pilate has before him two men, two accused political prisoners named Jesus. One of the prisoners is Jesus Barabbas, something documented only in Matthew's gospel. The other gospels refer to this man only as Barabbas. Whether Barabbas or Jesus Barabbas, this man is said to have been a notorious criminal, a murderer, and an armed insurrectionist. In our day, we would call him a terrorist (see John R.W. Stott's book *Cross of Christ*).

The other prisoner, of course, is Jesus, called the Messiah. Jesus of Nazareth.

I remember the first time it was pointed out to me that Pilate had the option of choosing between two prisoners who were named Jesus, and how each of us is given the opportunity to choose a Jesus who desires to bring about a different world through violence/terrorism against those in authority, or the Jesus who works to bring about a new world through peace.

That is something to ponder, to be sure.

But this morning, building on my time of preparation for this meditation, I cannot help but think of someone whose name we probably do not know, someone who is not present in the scene, yet someone whose message served as a warning then and an opportunity for us to reflect today.

I am talking, of course, about the wife of Pontius Pilate. The mention of her disappears as quickly and as subtly as it appears. This is Matthew 27:19: *While (Pilate) was sitting on the judgment seat, his wife sent word to him, 'Have nothing to do with that innocent man, for today I have suffered a great deal because of a dream about him.'*

Now, I do not claim that what I am about to present is an exhaustive, academic unpacking of this verse. But I am intrigued by the fact that God or an angel of the Lord (presumably) spoke to the wife of Pontius Pilate in a dream. There is precedent in Matthew's gospel for this. I find it hard to believe that it is a mere coincidence that an angel of the Lord speaks to persons in dreams immediately before important events regarding Jesus.

If we go back to the opening chapters of Matthew's gospel, we recall how an angel of the Lord spoke with Joseph, to whom Mary, the mother of Jesus, was betrothed. Remember, Joseph was going to break things off with Mary once he learned that Mary was pregnant, and the child was not his. But an angel of the Lord appeared to Joseph in a dream and assured him everything would be okay, and he could still take Mary as his wife (Matthew 1:18-25).

The angel would speak to Joseph in a dream after Jesus was born, instructing him to take Mary and the Christ-child to Egypt to escape the wrath of Herod, the Roman client king of Judea at the time of Jesus' birth.

We also learn that an angel of the Lord spoke with the Magi, the Wise Men, in a dream, warning them not to return to Herod the Great after encountering the Christ-child. Herod lied to the Magi, telling them he wanted to know the location of the baby Jesus so he, too, could worship Jesus. But the Magi saw through that lie, maybe (likely?) with the help of the angel's message in the dream.

As far as I can tell, there are no other references in Matthew's gospel to God speaking to people through dreams, until we get to Jesus' arrest more than thirty years later. The biblical text is unclear, but I am going out on a limb here and saying that an angel of the Lord spoke to the wife of Pontius Pilate in that dream.

What we do know from the text is that the wife of Pontius Pilate, whom some Christian traditions later referred to as Saint Claudia and/or Saint Procla, was convinced that Jesus of Nazareth was innocent. In addition, she mentions in the "word" to her husband that she suffered greatly because of the message communicated to her in the dream.

How did the wife of Pontius Pilate suffer when it dawned on her that Jesus was innocent?

This is pure speculation on my part, but I think the following questions are fair to ask:

Did the wife of Pontius Pilate know her husband was more inclined to appease a raucous crowd about Jesus of Nazareth than to make a sound decision, even when the truth was staring him in the face?

Did she know what Jesus would have to suffer if her husband sentenced Jesus to death by crucifixion?

Did she know she and her husband might later regret the verdict rendered against Jesus on that day?

Did the wife of Pontius Pilate eventually become a Christian? Is Saint Claudia, the wife of Pontius Pilate, the Claudia mentioned in the closing sentences of the Second Letter of Paul to Timothy? How did the gospel writers know so much about Jesus' time before Pontius Pilate? Did they hear about it from Claudia?

Both the gospels of Luke and John mention that Pontius Pilate declared publicly three times that he could find no basis for the charges of treason and sedition leveled against Jesus by the religious establishment (see Stott's *Cross of Christ*). Meaning, despite the fact that Pilate asked Jesus in John's gospel "what is truth," Pilate knew the truth about Jesus.

Whether Pilate was dismissive of the warning from his wife or saw it as confirmation of his gut instinct that Jesus was innocent, Pilate chose not to allow the truth about Jesus to influence his decisions about Jesus' future. What is worse, Pilate even declared himself innocent of Jesus' blood, soon to be shed on the Cross, a death Pilate could have prevented.

Pilate, maybe because of a deep need to be liked, was more concerned about his popularity before the crowds outside his palace than he was about his standing before God in human flesh. His politics took precedence over a life of faith. As a result, Pilate received the popularity he may have desperately craved. Christians have been reciting his name weekly, if not daily, pretty much ever since Pilate made the wrong decision about Jesus.

What about us?

What if we were ever put in the position of choosing between a Jesus of violence and a Jesus of peace?

Would we be swayed by a nearly riotous crowd or the lone voice of a trusted loved one who knows us better than we know ourselves?

CURTIS NORMAN

What would we do?

MAUNDY THURSDAY

March 28, 2024

We began tonight's Maundy Thursday liturgy with *An Exhortation* which is based on our patron, St. Paul's, theology of the Eucharist, as articulated in his First Letter to the Church in Corinth, Greece. Part of that epistle is in the assigned Lectionary for this evening.

Here is a fact I find somewhat curious, and I beg your indulgence as I get a bit nerdy. The Exhortation used to be required in Anglican celebrations of the Holy Eucharist, going back to the Prayer Books of 1549, 1552, 1662, and 1789 and I am going to return to that word "required" here in a bit because it is ever present, overtly or implied, in the Prayer Book where the *Exhortation and Catechism* are concerned.

In the Church's first four Prayer Books, a form of the Exhortation was recited at each service of Holy Communion. That changed a bit in the 1892 Prayer Book, where the Exhortation was "required" to be read only once a month. The rubrics changed a little more with the 1928 Prayer Book, where the Exhortation was "required" to be read on the First Sunday in Advent, the First Sunday in Lent, and Trinity Sunday only.

With the *1979 Book of Common Prayer*, which is what we use now, the Exhortation became optional; it was no longer required in the Church's worship. I find this strange, given that this Prayer Book, for the first time, stated that the principal worship service of the Episcopal Church is Holy Communion.

If Communion is to be celebrated every Sunday, and not just once a month or once a quarter, in addition to Christmas and Easter, would not it make sense for the Christian faithful to want to know how to get the most out of the experience?

How can the Eucharist be especially meaningful to you?

A lingering question for me is: even though we receive the Body and Blood of Christ quite often in the Episcopal Church, are we at risk of a decreased appreciation of what takes place in the celebration of the Holy Eucharist, resulting in a less devout, less potentially transformative experience for the Christian faithful?

Now, I am wandering into dangerous territory here.

Radical inclusivity is a hallmark of the Episcopal Church. We are increasingly careful not to exclude or offend anyone, especially when it comes to receiving the Sacrament, and rightfully so.

Who are we to deny anyone's access to God?

I want as many people as possible around God's table at St. Paul's because that is precisely what Jesus models.

But alongside this radical inclusivity there needs to be a rationale that undergirds it.

My hope for all people gathered around this table is that they understand as much as possible what is happening in the Holy Eucharist, and to receive the Sacrament in what the Prayer Book describes as–and here comes another tricky word–a "worthy" manner.

I think you have figured out from me by now that the last thing I want any of us to be is a mindless follower of Jesus.

This is where the *Exhortation* benefits us.

For one thing, the *Exhortation* calls us to remember the dignity of the Sacrament. The Eucharist is not the Church's wine and cheese reception, it is not on the same level as a beer and pizza party.

On Easter Sunday, the red wine cannot be replaced with white wine or champagne, which has been known to happen.

In the Eucharist, we receive the Body and Blood of Christ.

Saint Paul wrote that we would be receiving the Sacrament improperly if we failed to recognize that Christ is truly present in the bread and wine.

It is important to note that the Episcopal Church's *Exhortation* does not include (or even rule out, for that matter) a theology of transubstantiation, which our Roman Catholic brothers and sisters adhere to.

Episcopal theology simply accepts on faith that Christ is in the bread and wine of the Eucharist because Christ said he would be.

I can trust that Christ is truly present in the Sacrament without having to understand how that takes place.

At the same time, the Exhortation avoids the opposite, more Protestant extreme of Eucharistic theology, which contends that our celebrations of Holy Communion are simply a memorial.

This basically means that Jesus is not truly (physically) present in the Bread and Wine. And do not worry, if that describes your beliefs about Communion, that is fine. You'll understand why in a moment.

The Eucharist *is* a memorial, but the Prayer Book of the Episcopal Church teaches that Christ is truly present in the Eucharist.

Anglicanism/Episcopalianism seeks to carve out that middle way, the Via Media. There is the dignity of the Sacrament itself because Christ is truly present in the bread and wine, and it is okay to embrace the Mystery of the Eucharist without having to dissect it.

The *Exhortation* then turns to how we are to receive Holy Communion in a worthy manner. For this, we now go to the *Catechism*, which summarizes the next section of the Exhortation.

On page 860 of the Prayer Book, we read this:

Q.   What is required of us when we come to the Eucharist?
A.   It is required that we should examine our lives, repent of our sins, and be in love and charity with all people.

Let me now say a bit here about the word "required."

I am not sure how the word "required" sounds to your ears coming from a representative of a religious institution like me.

It sounds a bit legalistic and authoritarian to me, like we have to be good little boys and girls to get our milk and cookies.

Although the word "required" does not sound pastoral, I do believe the 1979 Prayer Book's intention here is pastoral.

I think the Episcopal Exhortation calls us to be mindful followers of Jesus.

We are to reflect seriously and prayerfully on the decisions we make daily. Be honest with ourselves and admit where we can do better in our lives and then endeavor to love everybody God puts in our path. Or, as Jesus puts it, to love one another as He loves us so that when we receive the broken Body and shed Blood of Christ, paradoxically, we are relieved to find out that a worthy reception of Holy Communion does not depend on our personal worthiness.

The Eucharistic celebration is God's grace: unmerited nourishment for this journey called life; manna from heaven that helps us become what we eat.

When we prepare, using the guidance of the *Exhortation* and *Catechism*, we are reminded that our reception of the Body and Blood of Christ in Holy Communion is worthy, not because we are living our lives perfectly, not because our Eucharistic theology is airtight. Our reception of Holy Communion is worthy only because the God who comes to us in Jesus invites us to share in His worthiness.

Because this is true, the only possible response to God's grace in Jesus Christ is "thank you."

It is indeed Holy Eucharist.

GOOD FRIDAY

March 29, 2024

I would like to reflect for just a moment on John 19:34. Jesus has died on the cross. Some members of the religious establishment have asked that the Roman soldiers remove Jesus' body from the cross, as well as the bodies of others who were being crucified with Jesus. They want the bodies removed because it is almost the Sabbath for persons of the Judaic faith. Sabbath begins at 6 pm on Fridays. And because of the significance of the Sabbath, especially on the Passover, nobody wants to look up from their dinner table only to see capital punishment.

This is horrible to say, but it needs to be said. Apparently, the two others who are being crucified with Jesus have not yet died. Nobody knows if they would die before 6 pm, the Sabbath, so the request is for the Roman soldiers to break the legs of the other two on the cross.

It seems that breaking the legs of a person being crucified speeds up their death. And that is exactly what the Roman soldiers do; they get the desired results. But they do not have to break the legs of Jesus. Jesus is already dead.

Just to make sure, one of the soldiers takes his spear and thrusts it into Jesus' side. The soldier gets the confirmation he was seeking. Jesus is dead. Blood and water flow out of the gash that the soldier has carved into Jesus' body.

Blood and water.

What is it, about blood and water?

People smarter than I can offer a medical explanation here as to why blood and water would have flowed from Jesus' body. But I am not a physician. So, I would like to reflect on blood and water theologically. I ask that you indulge me as I use my holy imagination. I invite you to use yours.

I am not sure the connection I will attempt to make can be understood as something John intended when he wrote his gospel. But here is what I have been thinking about lately: the blood and water of Jesus' body and the blood and water of the Exodus.

We know the story of the Exodus. God's chosen people, the Hebrews, were enslaved by Pharaoh in Egypt for more than 400 years. God empowered Moses, born a Hebrew slave, brought up as an Egyptian prince, to work through an existential/identity crisis to lead the Hebrews out of Egypt into the wilderness so that God's chosen people could ultimately reach the land God had promised them.

Yes, we know this story. But let's take a closer look. There is always more to learn.

In Exodus chapters three and four, Moses met God at the burning bush. God instructed Moses to go to Pharaoh and demand that Pharaoh let the Hebrews go. But Moses was afraid, not so much of Pharaoh, but of the possibility that the Hebrews would not believe that God had sent him (Moses) to liberate them.

To reduce Moses's anxiety, God instructed Moses to perform a few signs. The first was for Moses to throw his staff on the ground and watch it become a snake. The second was for Moses to put his hand in his cloak, and when Moses pulled his hand out of his cloak, it was leprous. Then, Moses followed God's instructions in reverse, and his hand was once again spotless. I bet Harry Potter's cloak couldn't do that.

God went on to say that IF the Hebrews watched Moses perform these signs and they still did not believe God sent him, Moses was to "...take some water from the Nile and pour it on the dry ground; the water that you shall take from the Nile will become blood on the dry ground" (Exodus 4:9).

Hold that thought.

Let's fast-forward to Exodus, chapter seven. Moses has implored Pharaoh to let the Hebrews be freed from slavery. Pharaoh refuses. So, here comes God with the first of the ten plagues to hopefully change Pharaoh's mind. What is the first plague?

God instructed Moses to say this to Pharaoh, and I quote the beginning from Exodus 7:14. This is Moses speaking:

"Thus says the Lord, 'By this you shall know that I am the Lord.' See, with the staff that is in my hand, I will strike the water that is in the Nile, and it shall be turned to blood. The fish in the river shall die, the river itself shall stink, and the Egyptians shall be unable to drink water from the Nile.'" The Lord said to Moses, 'Say to Aaron, "Take your staff and stretch out your hand over the waters of Egypt—over its rivers, its canals, and its ponds, and all its pools of water—so that they may become blood; and there shall be blood throughout the whole land of Egypt, even in vessels of wood and in vessels of stone."'

What is it with blood and water? What is the point of God having Moses turn the water of the Nile into blood?

Well, one theory is that the Nile River was the lifeblood of Egypt. It was the economic engine. God crippled Pharaoh's bank account by turning the water of the Nile into blood. The theory is valid.

But there is another theory, one I heard first from Rabbi David Fohrman. For this theory, we need to back up a bit in Exodus, chapter one. Pharaoh was concerned at how populous the Hebrews were becoming. Pharaoh was afraid that the Hebrews would team up with Egypt's enemies. So, Pharaoh, insecure and hoping to retain power, issued the following command. This is Exodus, chapter one, verse 22:

"Pharaoh commanded all his people, 'Every boy that is born to the Hebrews you shall throw into the Nile, but you shall let every girl live.'"

Notice: Pharaoh commanded all his people. Not just his soldiers. Every single Egyptian was empowered by the government to kill young Jewish boys. And that is what happened. Mass infanticide. It is not stated expressly. But we are talking here about water and blood.

From there, the book of Exodus goes on to explain how Moses was saved from ending up at the bottom of the Nile. But let's get back to the question.

What is it, about blood and water from the Nile River?

Remember what God said to Moses at the burning bush: if the Hebrews do not believe I sent you after the first two miracles, then take water from the Nile, pour it on the ground, and they will see blood.

Meaning, even though the Nile did not turn red every time an Egyptian tossed a Hebrew boy into the river, even though the currents of the Nile swept away the evidence of infanticide, even though the Nile still glistens in the sun, God saw what happened.

God saw the injustice that Pharaoh and his people inflicted on the Hebrews.

God saw the blood of every single innocent Hebrew newborn boy, the pain and grief it all caused for Hebrew families, and how those enslaved could easily think that God had forsaken them, and that God would never send someone to rescue them.

When the Hebrews saw Moses pour water from the Nile onto the ground, they saw the blood and knew beyond a shadow of a doubt that God had not forgotten them, and that Moses was, indeed, sent by God to liberate them.

Let's now return to John's gospel and focus on another Hebrew who escaped infanticide, ironically by being taken to Egypt.

Jesus has died on the cross. A Roman soldier has pierced Jesus' side to make sure he is dead. Blood and water flow from Jesus.

Is it possible that the blood and water flowing from Jesus is somehow connected to the blood and water of the Exodus?

I could be wrong. I probably am. And I will be the first to admit my error if someone can prove otherwise.

Until such time, in the midst of whatever enslaves us, in times when we think God has forgotten our life circumstances, in moments when we seem to have lost our hope and faith, I believe that the blood and water from the Body of Christ flowed to remind us that even in our darkest moments, when we are tempted to think that God has forsaken us, Jesus' death on the cross is evidence that God sees our plight and has not abandoned us.

EASTER SUNDAY

March 31, 2024

Alleluia! Christ is Risen!
The Lord is Risen Indeed! Alleluia!

I invite you to join me as we walk with Mary Magdalene this morning to the tomb where Jesus' body had been placed after Good Friday. I am working here from John's gospel in our bulletin insert, but I do want to note from Mark's gospel, the other passage we could have read this morning, that Mary Magdalene ventured to the tomb (with Mary, the mother of James and Salome) to anoint Jesus' body to attend to his death. The gravesite was not as Mary had expected. The huge stone that covered the entrance to the cave where Jesus' body was, well, that stone had been rolled away. That was quite a task to be accomplished.

Mary ran to find Simon Peter and John, the gospel writer who shares this morning's story with us. John refers to himself as the disciple whom Jesus loved. Let me just say that, at first glance, it would seem to be a statement of arrogance or pride on John's part. It is not. It was a description of great humility.

Peter and John race to the tomb, and Mary Magdalene goes with them. Both Peter and John enter the tomb but do not see Jesus' body, so they go back home.

Mary Magdalene, on the other hand, remains at the tomb. She is crying. She looks in the tomb and sees two angels who ask her, *"Woman, why are you weeping?"*

Her answer is straightforward: "They have taken away my Lord, and I do not know where they have laid him."

Mary then turns around and sees Jesus, but she does not know it is Jesus yet. The Risen Christ asks Mary, *"Woman, why are you weeping? Whom are you looking for?"*

Now, John adds something to his story that I find quite fascinating. It is this: Mary Magdalene thinks that Jesus is the gardener. So, we must ask, why did Mary think that the Risen Christ was the gardener? What was Jesus doing to make Mary Magdalene suppose that he was the gardener at the cemetery?

Well, to possibly answer this question with our holy imaginations, let's go back to the earliest part of the book of Genesis. God creates the first human and places him in the Garden of Eden. The first human's job was to till God's Garden. Adam was to take care of, to steward, God's good creation. Adam was to tend to life.

But we all know that the first Adam sinned. Adam and Eve thought they knew better than God how to cultivate life. Through their actions, their original sin, Adam and Eve put all of humanity at a distance from God. This is why God had to become human in the person of Jesus of Nazareth, to accomplish the work that humanity cannot do on its own, to bridge the divide that we put between ourselves and God.

So, when Mary Magdalene arrives at the tomb on that first Easter morning, the Risen Christ is already doing what he came to do. He was tilling God's Garden, stewarding God's good creation. The Risen Christ is tending to "life" in a cemetery, in a location where we expect to find only death.

But back to Jesus' question to Mary Magdalene: *"Woman, why are you weeping? Whom are you looking for?"*

Mary says: *"Sir, if you have carried him away, tell me where you have laid him, and I will take him away."*

Notice what happens next. The Risen Christ simply calls her name: "Mary!"

And that is all it takes for Mary to stop attending to death and begin tending God's life.

The voice of Jesus speaks Mary's name, and her eyes are opened to Resurrection!

It is important to point out here the significance of Resurrection life.

It is not entirely clear in the passage, but when Mary realizes that she is in the presence of the Risen Christ, she seems to have either grabbed Jesus by the arm or given him a bear hug. I think this because Jesus says to her: "Do not hold on to me because I have not yet ascended to the Father. But go to my brothers and say to them, 'I am ascending to my Father and your Father, to my God and your God.'"

What is going on here? Why does the Risen Christ implore Mary Magdalene not to hold on to him? I think this is a lynchpin of Resurrection life. Too often, when we think we are embracing Resurrection life, we are really clinging to our ideas about the past.

With Mary Magdalene, it is fair to ask if she wanted the Risen Jesus to return to what he was doing before the events of Holy Week and Good Friday.

But with Resurrection life, there is no going back, there is only going forward. Our mission and ministry is to tend life, especially in places where, at first glance, we only see death.

Good people of Saint Paul's Episcopal Church in Brady, Texas, let me get personal here for a moment.

When we approach this beautiful, holy campus at the corner of Blackburn and 11th, what thoughts go through our minds?

Do we think only of things that used to be?

Do we think Jesus' seven last words from the cross were: "We have never done it that way before?"

Do we want to cling to an idea of "how to do church" that has been obsolete since the 1980s?

Are we afraid that the best days of St. Paul's are behind us? If so, how sad are we about that?

If I have touched a nerve here, I have another question for you— maybe two questions, three, or four.

Why are you weeping? Whom are you looking for?

Are we attending to death when we should be tending God's life?

I have been with you for almost a year. I do not yet have a complete picture of what God is doing through His Holy Spirit, and what God's future for St. Paul's will look like.

But make no mistake.

God is clearly at work in the patch of His garden we call St. Paul's.

And God is calling each of us by name. So, instead of clinging to the past, let's fling our arms wide, and be open to God tending New Life!

Alleluia! Christ is Risen!
The Lord is Risen Indeed! Alleluia!

THE ASCENSION

May 9, 2024

Today is the Feast of the Ascension. It is 40 days after Easter Sunday, which is why we always commemorate the Risen Christ ascending to the right hand of God the Father on a Thursday (clearly everybody's favorite day to come to church).

As we have done before, I would invite us to reflect briefly on how Scripture talks about humanity's relationship with the God we know in Jesus Christ.

One way we understand our relationship with God comes through the imagery of walking.

For example, in the Book of Leviticus (26:3, 12), we hear God say to the Israelites:

If you follow my statutes and keep my commandments and observe them faithfully . . . I will walk among you and will be your God, and you shall be my people.

Humanity was created to walk with, to be in a relationship with God. When we walk with God, we mature, we become the people God created us to be, and we are empowered to help create the kind of world God desires.

But we know, too, from Scripture that humanity does not always walk perfectly with God, which changes the way we relate to God.

In Genesis 3, in the Garden of Eden, when Adam and Eve ate from the tree God commanded them to not eat from, their relationship with God was changed, and not in a good way. Adam and Eve consciously stopped walking with God.

They heard the sound of the Lord God walking in the garden at the time of the evening breeze, and the man and his wife hid from the presence of the Lord God among the trees of the garden. But the Lord God called to the man and said to him, 'Where are you?'

The original Hebrew does not translate well into English with God's question where are you. This is not so much a "where" in terms of location but a "where" in terms of lament. God says to Adam and Eve:

Why are you not where you should be? Why are you not walking with me in the garden like I had hoped you would be?

I now beg your pardon as I mix metaphors. We talk about humanity's relationship with God through the imagery of walking, but let's also think of it as riding a bike, a concept those in biblical times could not have imagined.

When we are intentional about our relationship with God, there are times when humanity needs training wheels. And there are times when God takes off the training wheels.

In the Garden of Eden, Adam and Eve needed the training wheels. Remember God's command to the first humans: you may eat from the billions of trees in the Garden, but do not eat from the Tree of the Knowledge of Good and Evil.

Lots of trees to eat from. Only one they could not eat from. Guess which one they ate from.

Now, there is a school of religious thought that speculates that the command not to eat from the Tree of the Knowledge of Good and Evil was not permanent. The idea is that Adam and Eve were supposed to eat from all the other trees before eating from the Tree of Good and Evil, prerequisites to eating from the Tree of Knowledge, dare we say, training wheels.

But Adam and Eve tried to ride a bike for the first time without training wheels, and they crashed.

God then had to remove Adam and Eve from the Garden so that humanity could start again. God put training wheels on Adam and Eve and rebooted the process of learning what it means to walk with God.

This process of learning culminates in the Incarnation of Jesus Christ, God taking on human flesh in the person of Jesus of Nazareth. Jesus walks among humanity for about 33 years, the last three publicly, teaching about the Kingdom of God, performing miracles, and freely choosing to die on the Cross to reconcile humanity to God the Father.

Jesus dies on the Cross, and there is an in-between space between Good Friday and Easter Sunday, a time between what was and what was to come.

Christ is then raised from the dead., His disciples have to learn how to relate to the Resurrected Christ in a new way, After forty days Christ ascends to the right hand of God the Father and there is, once again, an in-between space: ten days between the Ascension and Pentecost; ten days without the Risen Christ, and ten days without the Holy Spirit.

Immediately after Christ ascends, I would argue that the first apostles and disciples did something similar to what Adam and Eve did; because the Risen Christ had left their physical presence, the apostles/disciples experienced a change in the way they related to God, and they froze. They, like Adam and Eve, stopped walking with God. They did not want to ride their bikes without training wheels.

I mean, yes, Christ ascended to the right hand of God the Father. But where exactly is that? Where did Jesus go?

We ask that question now that the first followers of Jesus asked it two thousand years ago.

We read in Acts of the Apostles (1:9-11):

"... as they were watching, he was lifted up, and a cloud took him out of their sight. While he was going and they were gazing up towards heaven, suddenly, two men in white robes stood by them. They said, 'Men of Galilee, why do you stand looking up towards heaven? This Jesus, who has been taken up from you into heaven, will come in the same way as you saw him go into heaven.'"

The Apostles stood still looking up towards the sky. Maybe they were not so much looking for Christ as they were lamenting that Christ was not with them like he had been.

But what should the apostles have done? They should have kept walking with God, even though their relationship with God had taken a turn they were not expecting. And the apostles did start walking again when prompted by "two men in white robes," messengers from God, angels.

What followed was the first bishop's election on record.

Let me close with this, a question you might wish to ponder between now and Pentecost or anytime.

Why do we sometimes stop walking with God?

1) Like Adam and Eve, we sometimes stop walking with God because we realize we have done something wrong. What is worse: we try to hide from God because we think that because of our wrongdoing, we are not worthy of God's love and God's grace. But that is not true. God goes to great lengths to keep walking with us. Just ask Adam and Eve. So, that is one reason we sometimes stop walking with God: sin.

2) A second reason we might stop walking with God is that as we mature in the faith. As we grow closer to God and realize the responsibilities of discipleship we have to learn

to relate to God in new ways. We have to engage life in ways we never thought we would, ways which can be engaged only when we take off the training wheels. Taking off the training wheels can sometimes be scary, but it is also really exciting and life-giving.

As I reflect on where we are on the liturgical calendar and all that is taking place in our world, let alone the impending conclusion of a pastoral relationship at St. Paul's, God needs a Church that prepares for the training wheels to be removed.

Grant, we pray, Almighty God, that as we believe your only-begotten Son our Lord Jesus Christ to have ascended into heaven, so we may also in heart and mind there ascend, and with him continually dwell; who lives and reigns with you and the Holy Spirit, one God, for ever and ever. Amen.

MARK 6:34

July 21, 2024

From Mark's gospel, we learn:

(Jesus) saw a great crowd; and he had compassion for them, because they were like sheep without a shepherd; and he began to teach them many things.

Last Saturday evening, Margaret and I were at Mustang Island Camp and Conference Center, our diocesan camp in Port Aransas. It was during dinner that we learned of the attempted assassination of former President Trump. We spent much of the rest of the evening watching the news.

When I watch the news, I am always curious to hear how people speak about God in times of trauma, how we work through our grief, and how we try to make sense of life, even though not everything in this life makes sense.

Some of you may be aware that I have a keen interest in Christian Apologetics which examines the reasons and evidence that Christianity is true, rational, and worthy of belief, although this discipline has its limits.

I have studied apologetics for nearly 25 years but will never be an expert. Yet I have learned enough apologetics to recognize obvious errors about how the God we know in Jesus Christ interacts with humanity and all of creation.

Now, please hear what I am saying. I will try to speak clearly enough to prevent you from hearing something I am not saying. I ask for your grace and forgiveness in advance for any mistakes I do not intend to make.

I am not engaging in partisan American politics here. I am a Christian priest. My focus is theological and, ultimately, pastoral.

Over the past week, some have been going on the news and social media cherry-picking passages from the Bible and claiming that (and I am pretty much quoting here) God's hand was on President Trump and the "wind of the Holy Spirit" moved the bullet to save both the former president and the United States of America.

If that depiction of God's providence is consistent with what we know about the God revealed in Scripture–and I do not believe it is—then not only would it have been God's plan to save Donald Trump but a logical extension of that thought would result in God's hand not being on the husband, father, and firefighter who just happened to be behind Trump: the man who was killed by the bullet intended for the former president.

Furthermore, the hand of God would not have been on the two other people shot by the would-be assassin.

This is an appropriation of the Christian faith.

Why would I want to put my faith in a god who values the life of a person in high public standing more than that of an extraordinary, everyday person?

If this is what Christians supposedly believe about the God we know in Jesus, then what are we to make of President Biden saying the only thing that would get him to end his re-election bid is a personal visit from the Lord God Almighty himself?

These are just a couple of recent examples of how humanity has a long history of co-opting God to promote our own sinful agendas.

This is why I study apologetics.

What we believe about God matters. If we get the truth about God wrong, if we settle for mindless cliches, glib memes, and so-called biblical interpretation influenced by raw emotion and political bias, we violate the biblical Commandment not to take God's Name in vain.

Stated another way: "*You shall not make wrongful use of the name of the Lord your God, for the Lord will not acquit anyone who misuses his name.*"

When we misrepresent God, we dishonor God, mislead others, and open ourselves to God's judgment.

Truth matters.

And when I say "truth," part of what I mean is this: truth, by definition, is exclusive.

Let me say that again: truth, by definition, is exclusive.

At the most basic level, for something to be true, something else has to be false. Yet that is not what we are told in our culture.

We live in a culture where people claim there is my truth, your truth, somebody else's truth, and what is true for me does not necessarily need to be true for you. When we buy into the lie that there are equal and therefore competing truths, we employ force to win the day of the ideals to which we subscribe.

But when we use our brains and think critically, common sense tells us that not everything can be true.

Therefore, instead of playing fast and loose with the Bible, it is critical for us to intelligently mine the depths of the truth God reveals to us fully in Jesus of Nazareth, and work diligently to discern how to correctly apply Christ's truth to every aspect of our lives.

***

At the risk of hubris, I wonder if God is currently looking at our nation in the same way Jesus looked at the crowd in this morning's gospel passage.

Jesus felt sorry for the crowd. He had compassion for them because they were like sheep without a shepherd: rudderless, directionless, aimless, and therefore vulnerable, easily exploitable, and ignorant of their commodification.

Think about the shepherds we read about in this morning's passage from the Prophet Jeremiah:

Woe to the shepherds who destroy and scatter the sheep of my pasture! says the Lord. Therefore thus says the Lord, the God of Israel, concerning the shepherds who shepherd my people: It is you who have scattered my flock, and have driven them away, and you have not attended to them.

The passage goes on to say:

The days are surely coming, says the Lord, when I will raise up for David a righteous Branch, and he shall reign as king and deal wisely, and shall execute justice and righteousness in the land. In his days Judah will be saved and Israel will live in safety. And this is the name by which he will be called: "The Lord is our righteousness.

When we read this passage from Jeremiah along with Mark's gospel noticing there are false shepherds and *one* good shepherd, we are to understand beyond the shadow of a doubt that Jesus of Nazareth is the righteous Branch.

Jesus is the Good Shepherd spoken of in the 23rd Psalm.

So, the question then becomes: How does Jesus begin to shepherd the crowd we meet in this morning's gospel passage?

Mark gives us the answer with an economy of words. Mark says that Jesus "began to teach them many things."

Jesus began to teach the crowd many things. But what did Jesus teach the crowd? Mark does not elaborate here so we must consider the truth we have learned about Jesus to this point in Mark's gospel.

If we go back to chapter one, we hear the words of God the Father at Jesus' baptism where he says: "You are my Son, the Beloved; with you I am well pleased." I believe we can faithfully infer that Jesus would have taught the crowd his identity, how the kingdom of God was now in their midst, and that people would have to repent, to turn 180 degrees, to move away from false shepherds, and commit their lives to following the Good Shepherd, the One who will say in John's gospel that he is the way, the truth, and the life, the One who teaches us not only to love God and our neighbors as we love ourselves, but to love our enemies, as well.

This past week is a prime example of how, even though Christians across the spectrum strive to follow Jesus' teachings, we still find it difficult to love our enemies, whether they are across the political aisle or the center aisle at Church.

Yet, truth matters. If Jesus commands us to love our enemies, we are to love our enemies no matter the personal cost.

The truth about Jesus. what God has revealed about Himself in Jesus, should impact how we live our lives even when, especially, when we find the truth challenging to integrate.

Truth requires that we let go of the lies we tell ourselves and grasp what God reveals to us in Jesus.

Discipleship is not simply a matter of knowing data about Jesus; the Christian enterprise is about integrating the truth about Jesus into our lives.

"Right belief" should give birth to "right practice," an integrity of faith.

***

As we navigate the political conventions and look ahead to November, we may be tempted to think that controlling the White House and Capitol Hill is the ultimate battle and that the only options are to "make America great again" or "build America back better."

But these options do not even come close to being helpful when we consider who God is calling the Church to be.

When I die, my soul is not going to Washington, DC.

So, when the Church hoists the banners of American politics higher than we lift the Cross, we sin; we abdicate God's unique call on our lives.

We must correct course and return to doing what the Church is designed to do for the world.

Repent. The Kingdom of God is at hand.

Believe the Good News. Be transformed by the power of the Holy Spirit.

Be guided daily by the truth revealed fully in *the* Good Shepherd, Jesus of Nazareth.

JOHN 6:1-21

July 28, 2024

Well, probably like every preacher in the pulpit this morning, I find there is no shortage of news items on which to comment. Because Jesus performs in our assigned passage from John's gospel, I had initially planned to begin this sermon by quoting legendary sports broadcaster Al Michaels from the 1980 Winter Olympics. When Team USA stunned the Soviet Union in hockey, Michaels famously exclaimed: "Do you believe in miracles?"

But then, on Friday, the opening ceremonies in Paris happened, and I have had to do a bit of editing in advance of reflecting on this passage from John's gospel.

You will notice right away that the lectionary has moved us from Mark's gospel to John's, and we will be hearing from John for the next several weeks. We will get back to Mark on Labor Day weekend.

Even though we have switched from Mark to John, there is a continuity between the story we had last week and the passage we have this morning. Last Sunday's passage from Mark extended from chapter 6, verses 30 through 34, and then we jumped to verses 53 through 56.

We skipped over two events last week, but we have them today: Jesus' feeding of the five thousand (or more) and Jesus' walking on water—two miracles from Jesus. We have John's versions of the events this morning.

Here is a question: why did Jesus perform miracles?

Some might even ask why God the Father does not perform miracles today in the same way that Jesus the Son did two thousand years ago. But the second question assumes that God does not work miracles anymore. Is that a correct assumption?

Could it possibly be that we have become too sophisticated to experience God's miracles? Have our hearts been hardened like Pharaoh's? Meaning, have we explained away the mysteries of God through our so-called enlightenment so that our skepticism comes naturally?

That is part of what it means when we read in Exodus that God hardened Pharaoh's heart. Pharaoh had resisted God's commands through Moses to free the Hebrews so often that it had become an automatic response to say no to God, and that is true for all of humanity.

When we resist God repeatedly, there comes a point in time when it takes no effort to resist God. Our hearts become hardened, and we close ourselves off from God's grace, mercy, love, and kindness.

Is it possible that our culture has hardened its hearts to God's miraculous works in our lives?

Here is what we need to know about Jesus' miracles, regardless of whether we are talking about Mark's gospel or John's or, for that matter, Matthew's or Luke's. Jesus performs these signs while teaching about his identity, how he is God in human flesh: the One who has come into the world to reconcile humanity to God.

Let me say something about this concept of identity. It is quite the buzzword in our day: identity.

What is the locus, the source of human identity?

According to ancient Jewish teaching– and remember, Jesus was Jewish–God created 974 generations before Adam and Eve. These people supposedly had the same physical and mental capabilities as humans today, but they lacked the divine soul that made them human beings. And because they sinned, because they chose their own ways over God's, God destroyed those generations. That is how the story goes.

Also, according to some Jewish traditions, Adam was the first created being to have a spiritual dimension, which includes the ability to love in the same way that God loves.

We know from Scripture that God said it wasn't good for Adam to be alone.

So, God created all of the animals in an attempt to find a suitable helper for Adam. When no suitable helper was found among all the animals God created, God took a rib, or more accurately, a side, from Adam and created woman, and the two were naked and unashamed.

As long as we are exploring various Jewish traditions, there is another which says the serpent was jealous that he was NOT chosen as the suitable helper for the first human. After all, the serpent was "more crafty" than any of the other animals that the LORD God had made. The Hebrew word for "crafty" has the same root as the Hebrew word for "naked," which means that the serpent was "more naked" (more passionate/less inhibited) than any other animals. But being the most human-like of all the animals was not enough for the serpent, and that sent the serpent into a rage (hissy fit?).

According to the tradition, the serpent plotted to kill Adam, marry Eve, and rule the Garden of Eden, but that did not work out for the serpent as planned and God punished the serpent to crawl the earth on his belly for the rest of existence, making us wonder whether the serpent, like humans, stood upright on two legs prior to the fall.

But what does this mean? What is the point of this Jewish

midrash, and why is it essential to our understanding of human identity, what it means to be created in the image of God? We might even go so far as to ask: what is the difference between a person and a snake?

Well, here is the thing with serpents, about all reptiles, and about all other animals that God has created.

Animals act solely on instinct (ever heard of the reptilian brain?), animals cannot harness their desires. Even the serpent, who was as close as an animal could get to being human without being human, acted without discernment: the serpent could do nothing but cave into its desires.

This is precisely the temptation the serpent presents to Eve and Adam: those desires you have, just give into them. Take this fruit. Yeah, God told you not to eat it, but it is okay to ignore God; you do not need God anymore, you can make your own choices, you do not need God to define you.

Do you see why the serpent could never be a suitable helper for humanity?

The serpent successfully tempted the first humans to be less than human. They did not discern proper human behavior in light of what God had spoken to them. They did not learn to channel their creative energies in godly ways. They sought to craft their own identity while rejecting God's in the process.

This is why we need to remember that we are created in the image of God and instead of caving into our base desires every chance we get, we are called to grow into the likeness of God; we are invited to choose love in the same way God chooses to love us; to live lives of holiness; we are to be set apart, different from the culture around us.

How do we do that?

The answer: Jesus.

Jesus is not just one teacher among many the world has known, and Christianity is not just one religion among many.

Jesus is the standard which is precisely why the Judeo-Christian tradition is often mocked.

In Jesus, through his birth, teaching, life, death, resurrection, ascension, and eventual return, we are given a tangible example of how we are to order our lives.

In Scripture, Jesus is called the Son of Man, a phrase we understand as the "ideal human."

Our patron, Saint Paul, called Jesus the New Adam.

God took on flesh in the person of Jesus of Nazareth to give us the prototype of how we are to live as human beings.

If Jesus is not fully God and fully human and if Jesus is not the objective standard, then the truth to which we aspire, it would not make sense to spend our Sunday mornings here, let alone commit our lives to him.

All of this is to say that the miracles we read about in Scripture are not the end in themselves. Miracles are a means to an end; they are signs pointing to a greater reality.

Jesus performed miracles to underscore his identity as God in human flesh to let us know that he is the standard by which, the foundation on which, we are to build our lives.

We grow into the identity that God designs for each and every one of us, what our Service of Baptism refers to as the Full Stature of Christ, when we use the brains God has given us to think critically about life and faith, and then choose to surrender our whole selves to Jesus, to model for the world that there is a better way to live.

JOHN 6:24-35

August 4, 2024

In John's gospel, the people ask Jesus:

"What must we do to perform the works of God?"

Jesus answered them, "This is the work of God, that you believe in him whom he has sent."

What must we do to perform the works of God? As I understand this question, it is like asking: Why am I here? What is the meaning of life? How am I supposed to live my life? Where is this out-of-control world heading?

These are the big issues of life: origin, meaning, morality, and destiny.

I do not know how successful I am. But my hope as your priest is that I can help cultivate an atmosphere at St. Paul's where it is safe for you to ask the big questions of life. If you do not feel like this is a place to ask and debate the hard questions in healthy ways, then I am not doing my job.

It is no surprise to anyone that our culture has long since lost its ability to engage in civil discourse. Social media is partly to blame for this. We can bunker down in silos with people who already agree with what we think; we do not have conversations across the divide. We simply shout our stances and refuse to listen to others who might challenge the status quo in which we take comfort. The institutional church certainly is not immune to this sort of behavior. We are sinful people, too.

But where the Church should differ from the world is that we should be able to argue without demonizing or turning those with whom we disagree into enemies. There are countless places in the Bible where people argue with God, even disengaging from God and others so that they can reflect, process, and better engage.

Jesus' disciples argued with one another all the time. I will never know how Jesus kept that group together. But he did because unity was/is important.

There was a famous dispute and split among the early Church, which is mentioned in Acts of the Apostles, chapter 15. Can you believe that? The Church talked about its problems. Here is what we know:

After some days, Paul said to Barnabas, 'Come, let us return and visit the believers in every city where we proclaimed the word of the Lord and see how they are doing.' Barnabas wanted to take with them John called Mark. But Paul decided not to take with them one who had deserted them in Pamphylia and had not accompanied them in the work. The disagreement became so sharp that they parted company; Barnabas took Mark with him and sailed away to Cyprus. But Paul chose Silas and set out, the believers commending him to the grace of the Lord. He went through Syria and Cilicia, strengthening the churches.

Fortunately, we know from Paul's first letter to the Corinthians that he and Barnabas reconciled and ministered together. We also learn from Paul's first letter to Timothy that Paul had once again found John Mark useful in the ministry.

Reconciliation happened. I wish I knew more about how the reconciliation came about, but it is clear that Paul did reconcile with both Barnabas and John Mark.

I do not need to see a show of hands or anything like that. But I wonder if you have ever experienced friction with another person or people in your life? More specifically, for our purposes here, I wonder if you have had a rough go of it while serving in church leadership, whether on a vestry or some other church board, this church or another.

I have been in the Episcopal Church my entire life. I am grateful for this denomination, although I try not to idolize it as I once did. I have wonderful memories. There have been times when I have been profoundly wounded by the institutional Church. And I have no doubt that I have inflicted wounds on others.

Disagreement is inevitable, emotions sometimes run high, because (if we are doing what a church is supposed to be doing) we engage in the arduous task of asking life's most important questions:

Why am I here? What is the meaning of life? How am I supposed to live my life? Where is this out-of-control world heading?

What must we do to perform the works of God?

Think about how serious this question is. Am I doing everything God would have me do? Am I doing it the right way? If I am doing it the wrong way, how will I know?

What must we do to perform the works of God?

The answer to this question is: believe in Jesus.

Place Jesus at the center of life. Make Jesus our priority.

Have faith in Jesus.

Trust that what Jesus shows us and teaches us about life will translate into more robust, deeper, impactful lives for each and every one of us!

Well, on the surface, that answer looks basic: believe in Jesus. But we all know that endeavoring to live our lives in light of what God has revealed to us in Jesus can be challenging.

If life was all easy-peasy, Saint Paul would not have had to write the following words to Christians in the city of Ephesus:

"I … beg you to lead a life worthy of the calling to which you have been called, with all humility and gentleness, with patience, bearing with one another in love, making every effort to maintain the unity of the Spirit in the bond of peace."

Why should we heed Paul's words? Because this is how God relates to us in Jesus: Christ came to us in humility and gentleness; He is patient with us; God in Christ Jesus stays in relationship with us; He keeps His end of the bargain even when we fail to live up to our end of the bargain.

Beyond the question of "why" we should live as Paul describes, there naturally arises the question of "how?"

We might phrase the question: How will believing in Jesus sustain us as we try to figure out this thing called life? The people asked Jesus the same question:

"What sign are you going to give us then so that we may see it and believe you? What work are you performing? Our ancestors ate the manna in the wilderness; as it is written, 'He gave them bread from heaven to eat.'"

Jesus answered by saying that He is the true bread of God, giving life to the world. When Jesus proclaims that He is the bread of life, he is saying that He is the lens that helps us see clearly the truth of how we got here, what this all means, how we fit in, and where we are going!

When the crowds around Jesus two thousand years ago heard Him say this, they said to Him:

"Sir, give us this bread always."

This is precisely why we approach the altar rail each and every Sunday to receive the Bread and Wine, the Body and Blood of Christ.

Like the crowd around Jesus long ago, we need nourishment for this journey called life, that movement from bondage to freedom, from death to life.

When we receive the Sacrament– an act in which each of us proclaims that we believe in Jesus–the word Sacrament itself comes from the Latin word *sacramentum*, which means "oath of allegiance," which is to say that when we receive the Sacrament, we are pledging our allegiance to Jesus Christ, and we invite the Holy Spirit to shape our morality as we engage the important questions of life.

When we receive the Sacrament, while we focus vertically on our relationship with God in Christ, we cannot help but notice the horizontal relationships. We see out of the sides of our eyes who else is receiving the Body and Blood of Christ: people we love, people we may disagree with, people about whom we might be skeptical, people who might be skeptical of us.

But there we are. Together. Kneeling before Christ.

When we approach the altar rail, those things that seek to divide us are rendered irrelevant in light of the unity Christ creates through the Sacrament.

When we receive the Body and Blood of Christ, we are reminded of what is truly important in life and are empowered to welcome God's kingdom into our midst.

What must we do to perform the works of God?

Believe in the one whom God has sent.

Believe in Jesus.

ANGER AND FORGIVENESS

August 11, 2024

In a few moments, we will sing the classic hymn *Rock of Ages*. The second verse begins this way: "Not the labors of my hands can fulfill thy law's demands."

It is an admission on our part that when we endeavor to do good works, we do so, not to earn our way into God's good graces. No, we do good works as a "response" to God's love for us in Jesus Christ.

It is important to understand that Christianity is not a meritocracy. Think of how often we have to earn the respect of our co-workers, the people in our community, or our teachers. That is a good thing in the community of Brady. There is a sense in which we have to earn our keep.

But we do not derive our self-worth from what we do in the eyes of others.

Our self-worth comes from being created in the image of God, and because we are created in the image of God, God invites us, in Christ, through the power of the Holy Spirit, to grow into God's likeness, to mature, to grow into the full stature of Christ, as we heard in the last week's section from Paul's letter to the Ephesians.

God acts first... and we are invited to respond.

So, in whatever good actions we choose, we need to understand that we are responding to God's love for us in Jesus Christ. We are not trying to earn God's love.

With that in mind, we reflect on St. Paul's instructions to Christians in the Church of Ephesus, a city in what is now Turkey. The highlights are as follows:

- Anger is a natural emotion, but when we get angry, be careful not to sin
  - There is plenty in this world to be angry about
  - But God in Christ calls us to learn how to channel our anger into something positive
- In our relationships with one another, build up and do not tear down
  - This may be enough to encourage us to delete all our social media accounts
  - We won't, but just think about what it is we post online in the heat of the moment
- Do not grieve the Holy Spirit (do not engage in willful disobedience to God)
- Forgive one another as God has forgiven you in Christ
  - If someone does us wrong, turn it over to God. Do not let others live rent-free in our head
  - As the old saying goes, unforgiveness is like drinking poison and expecting the person who did us wrong to die.

So, be angry but do not sin. Build up and do not tear down. Do not grieve the Holy Spirit. Forgive others as God has forgiven us.

When I think about these highlights, I think of the pattern that emerges from the book of Genesis. The late Rabbi Jonathan Sacks often spoke of how the book of Genesis is a story of sibling rivalries.

Early on in Genesis, we learn about the brothers Cain and Abel. Cain became jealous of Abel because God accepted Abel's religious offering instead of Cain's. The best we can infer from this is that

Cain did not offer God his best. Still, this made Cain angry. God warned Cain not to let his anger get the better of him, but he did, and he murdered his brother Abel. In this story of sibling rivalry, the dispute ended in fratricide.

You might be thinking, "Hang on, Fr. Curt. I would never murder anybody." True, but have we ever engaged in "cancel culture," which is our society's attempt at justice? The problem is that "cancel culture" looks nothing like God's justice, because "cancel culture" lacks grace.

Then there is the story of Ishmael and Isaac, half-brothers, sons of Abraham. In their case, the mothers were at each other's throats. Hagar (Ishmael's mother) was enslaved to Sarah, Abraham's wife and half-sister. But we will save that for another time.

While God promised a child to Abraham through Sarah, Sarah did not really believe at first that she could get pregnant in her old age, so she came up with a plan for Abraham to have a child with her slave girl, Hagar.

When Hagar got pregnant and gave birth to Ishmael, Sarah got jealous and tried to send Hagar and Ishmael away only to have that plan foiled by God.

When Sarah eventually gave birth to Isaac, she was worried that Ishmael would hurt him, so there was even more friction. There was tension the entire time.

But, fast-forwarding through the story, when Abraham died both Isaac and Ishmael were at his funeral. Meaning, that in this case of sibling rivalry, there was a form of tolerance of one another when all was said and done.

I do not believe tolerance is as virtuous as some in our culture make it out to be. Stay with me.

Then there is the rivalry between Isaac and Rebekah's twin sons, Esau and Jacob. Esau was the firstborn, and Jacob entered this world holding onto Esau's heel. The name Jacob means heel grabber. For most of his life, he lived up to his name; he was always pulling others down to raise himself up. But after many decades, again, making a long story short, there is a tempered reconciliation between Jacob and Esau.

Then, as part of the rivalry between Jacob's wives, Rachel and Leah (who were sisters) were also Jacob's cousins. But we will have to leave that for another time. There is a large amount of dissent between Jacob's son Joseph and his ten older brothers (sons of Leah, whom Jacob did not love as much as he loved Rachel).

You may have seen the musical *Joseph and the Amazing Technicolor Dreamcoat*. Joseph was the oldest son of Jacob's favorite wife, Rachel. Rachel had died, which had only elevated Joseph's standing in Jacob's eyes. Joseph was a jerk to his older brothers, so they sold him into Egyptian slavery and lied to their father, allowing Jacob to believe that Joseph had died.

When in Egypt, long story short, Joseph worked his way up the ladder in the Pharaoh's house. A famine strikes the land where Joseph's brothers are living. They travel to Egypt to secure food, and their fate is held in Joseph's hands, although they do not recognize the brother they sold into slavery.

When Joseph lets his brothers know who he is, they become afraid that he will retaliate for all the wrong they did to him. But the key line in Genesis here is: "What you meant for evil, God meant for good."

The final story of sibling rivalry in Genesis ends with full reconciliation.

If you ever grieve the Holy Spirit by wondering if God can bring new life out of your dysfunctional family, read Genesis. They are messed up and engage in actions for the sake of evil, yet God brings good out of it all.

When we think about it, this is the mission that God takes on in

Jesus Christ.

Humanity distances itself from God through sin.

God comes to us in Jesus. Jesus teaches us how to live, Jesus dies on the Cross to pay the penalty for sin that we cannot, and Jesus is raised from the dead on the third day to break down the barrier that we have erected against God.

God also sends the Holy Spirit to direct us in our everyday lives.

The Holy Spirit empowers us to, in the words of Paul, imitate God.

That is why we are here, to learn how to imitate the God we know in Jesus. The Church needs to do its part to end all the world's rivalries, one rivalry at a time.

Now, I have no way of knowing if Paul saw the pattern of sibling rivalry we now see in the book of Genesis. That maturing from fratricide, to tolerance, to tempered reconciliation, to complete reconciliation.

But I have no doubt that Paul understood what it meant for the churches of his day to seek the full stature of Christ.

This is our response to God's love for us in Christ Jesus:

Put away from you all bitterness and wrath and anger and wrangling and slander, together with all malice, and be kind to one another, tenderhearted, forgiving one another, as God in Christ has forgiven you. Therefore be imitators of God, as beloved children, and live in love, as Christ loved us and gave himself up for us, a fragrant offering and sacrifice to God.

SACRIFICE

August 18, 2024

From the Book of Proverbs, we read:

> *Come, eat of my bread*
> *and drink of the wine I have mixed.*
> *Lay aside immaturity and live,*
> *and walk in the way of insight.*

These are the words of a poetically personified Wisdom. God, of course, is the source of all wisdom. I am drawn to this little excerpt, and, more specifically, the final two lines, knowing full well that Wisdom here is speaking to, quote, "those without sense." Maybe a more positive way to say this would be that Wisdom is speaking to those who wish to make sense of this life.

As Christians, we are called to grow into the maturity we see in Jesus of Nazareth's life. We are to both live and walk in the way of insight.

We are to think critically about the life God has given us and all the challenges we encounter.

We should not just think about what is going on in the world around us but also respond in ways that God would have us.

In other words, our faith in Jesus should not be shallow. Our faith is not for show.

We are not here for style, but substance. We are talking about the Bread of Life.

We need to feast on this Bread and not settle for crumbs.

One of the areas we need to examine critically is the character of God and how God's character impacts our own character, our own morality and ethics.

Maybe you have encountered people in life who have said something like: "I would never believe in a God who allows so much suffering in this world."

This statement challenges God's character. It is an arrogant statement because it assumes that an individual person or the human race can have a stronger moral compass than God.

But it is also a popular sentiment, if not a roadblock for many people. Some are quite troubled by all the violence they see, not only in daily life, but in the Bible. They will point to a story like the one in Genesis (22), where God calls on Abraham to take his son Isaac up a mountain and kill and sacrifice him as part of a religious rite.

But the problem is that many people, while making a judgment about God because of this story, do not take the time to understand the context of the passage. Rabbis, philosophers, and Christian theologians have reflected on this story over the millennia and have even taken the ending of the story at face value where God stops Abraham from killing Isaac.

In Abraham's day, he was surrounded by cultures that sacrificed their children to whatever god they worshipped.

People killed their children ostensibly to better their own lives.

The Akedah, as this story is called, is a cautionary tale for people like me, as an agent of an institutional church, not to metaphorically sacrifice my children on the altar of my career.

My family always takes priority over my vocation. I can always walk away from the priesthood, but I will never walk away from my family in order to worship God.

Abraham had to learn a similar lesson and that is precisely why this story is in the Bible.

God does not require us to sacrifice our children to make Him happy. No, as Abraham told Isaac. as Isaac was becoming wise to what awaited him at the top of the mountain, Abraham responded: "God will provide the Lamb."

God will provide the sacrifice that we could never make.

And if people do not point to that story in their objection to God, they will quickly jump to God's command to the Israelites to commit genocide against the Canaanites so that the Israelites can take possession of the Promised Land.

But again, that is a surface-level summary of what happened, and such shallow treatments of this story are employed today with respect to certain geopolitical events. For one thing, there are times when the biblical writers use hyperbole. In this case, while war is commanded, the word annihilate is used much in the same way that today we would say:

During the regular season, every NFL team annihilates the Dallas Cowboys every Sunday.

That does not mean the Dallas Cowboys no longer exist, it just means they are not any good.

If they get past the first round of the playoffs, I will stop using the Cowboys as an example.

But wait just one minute, Father Curt. What did God have against the Canaanites?

Well, here is the thing we alluded to a moment ago. The Canaanites worshiped a god named Molech. Here is how the Canaanites worshiped Molech. The religion of Molech required that each family burn alive one of their children. And since, as we learned with Abraham and Isaac, God does not require child sacrifice, God wanted this practice to stop.

If we look closely, we notice how God was being gracious, because God had given the Canaanites warnings over the course of 400 years to stop killing their children (Genesis 15:13-16). When they did not stop, God ordered the Israelites to take action to save children.

Okay, Father Curt, but I still have a problem. If God does not take delight in parents killing their children, then why did God the Father murder God the Son on the Cross?

Think of the first line of this morning's Collect of the Day:

"Almighty God, you have given your only Son to be for us a sacrifice for sin …".

To some this sounds horrible, which means it is another matter that requires wisdom, discernment, and critical thinking.

This is where our theology of the Trinity comes into play. God is three distinct persons in one divine substance.

While Christ is God, Christ is not the Father or the Holy Spirit. So, when the Second Person of the Trinity (Christ) took on human form in Jesus of Nazareth, Jesus the Christ had personal agency.

Jesus freely chose to die on the Cross.

Jesus was not coerced by God the Father or God the Holy Spirit.

God the Father did not murder God the Son.

Christ Jesus accepted this charge.

Jesus is the Lamb that Abraham had faith God would provide!

In John's gospel, Jesus is quoted as saying:

For this reason the Father loves me, because I lay down my life that I may take it up again. No one takes it from me, but I lay it down of my own accord. I have authority to lay it down, and I have authority to take it up again. This charge I have received from my Father (John. 10:17-18).

Far from God the Father committing violence against God the Son, what we witnessed on Calvary was God at God's best and humanity at our worst.

So, if (after considering these Bible passages) I am still skeptical of God because of what I claim to be the violence of God, how arrogant am I?

Some are all too quick to blame God for all that is wrong in the world. But it is not God who is violent in the presence of humanity, it is humanity who is violent in the presence of God.

When I watch the news, and I admit that I watch the news way too much (but I am a news junkie, and I find much of this fascinating when I detach myself emotionally), I do not like what I see. I do not like the way people treat each other. I have developed a cynical view of national politics. I am disgusted with people on both sides of the aisle who are more concerned about themselves than us.

And I am being generous here with my words.

But when I watch the news, I am quickly reminded of the God who loves us (you and me) in Jesus, the Jesus we are called to imitate and proclaim.

This God loves us not always because of us, but oftentimes in spite of us, and God's self-giving love demands from us a particular response, which is why we pray in the Stations of the Cross:

Christ Jesus, though He was in the form of God, did not count equality with God a thing to be grasped; but emptied Himself, taking the form of a servant, and was born in human likeness. And being found in human form He humbled Himself and became obedient unto death, even death on a cross.

Therefore God has highly exalted Him, and bestowed on Him the name which is above every name.

Come, let us bow down, and bend the knee, and kneel before the Lord our Maker, for He is the Lord our God.

REVERENT KARAOKE

August 25, 2024

In just a moment, I will share a story about how our final hymn this morning came to be included in the Episcopal Hymnal. Before that, I would like to give an overview of how we approach music here at St. Paul's.

Like many other rural Episcopal congregations across the country, things are not like they used to be. I know there was a time when St. Paul's had an organist and a choir, and there was a time when Carol Reigner would plug her computer into the sound system, an organ would come out of the speakers, and Carol would lead all of you in singing.

Carol sent me an email this week. She recently got a new computer and once she has cleared most of the files off her old computer, she will send it to us with those music recordings.

What Carol did was quite a feat of ingenuity and has helped set the foundation for what we do currently with my iPhone what I would like to call "reverent karaoke." The recordings help us accomplish our goal for music at St. Paul's, which is congregational singing. That is the foundational purpose for music in the Church. We are to sing our faith in Jesus Christ.

The goal is not necessarily to have an organist or other live musicians because, a lot of times, what can happen is the live musician morphs into an entertainer. And that is not what we want. This is worship, not a concert.

Would I like to have an organist or a pianist? Of course. But we need to be realistic. Barring a miracle on par with the Virgin Birth, we will not find an Episcopal organist in McCulloch County or be able to afford one driving from Austin or San Antonio.

I believe God can perform such a miracle. Until that happens, we will be who we are and who we are is directly related to our adherence to the *Prayer Book, The Hymnal 1982*, and their supplements. The best way we can implement this plan right now is to have our congregational singing supported by recordings of the organ and choir.

As part of singing, we have some requirements for hymns.

For one thing, the words we sing in hymns need to be consonant with the story of the Bible and what the Church believes about God. Not every hymn or so-called Christian praise song released by professional artists fulfills that requirement.

Also, we will do our best to use hymns that are singable. Now and then, a tune accompanying a particular text must be learned. And that is okay. But just because we do not sing something well the first time we use it, it does not mean the hymn is not singable, it simply means we need to learn that hymn. We have one or two such hymns this morning, and I will get to that in a moment.

As I said, we will draw as much as possible on our Episcopal/ Anglican heritage. There are a lot of good hymns in our Episcopal Hymnal. There are some bad ones, in my opinion. And as much as we will draw on this heritage, I believe it is more than okay to add to our musical repertoire from other Christian traditions, whether Lutheran, Methodist, Presbyterian, Baptist, or Catholic, especially since the Episcopal Church continues to enter into "full communion" agreements with other denominations.

I mean, some of those Lutheran hymns are stout which I find ironic, given all the German ales and lagers!

And I have to say: we are doing this legally. We have secured the proper copyright licenses for printing the hymns in the bulletins and streaming them online, even though our online audio for music is not that great: all the more reason to worship at St. Paul's in person.

***

If you are an Anglophile, if you are a fan of things English, then you may have recognized our opening hymn. The lyrics are possibly new to you. But I would suspect the tune is at least somewhat familiar. If you watched the coronation of King Charles, or the funeral of Queen Elizabeth, or Harry and Megan's wedding, or remember Princess Diana's funeral, possibly even Grantchester, then you have heard this tune before.

The tune is called Thaxted, and it was composed by Englishman Gustav Holst. The tune is based on the middle section of "Jupiter" in his work *The Planets*. Holst adapted the music for lyrics written by Cecil Spring Rice which resulted in the hymn *I Vow to Thee My Country*: meaning, England. We cannot use those lyrics here in the U.S. much like we do not sing *God Save the King* when we hear the tune for *My Country Tis of Thee*.

Then, we have this morning's closing hymn, which you will see on the back page of the bulletin. It is number 597 in *The Hymnal 1982*. Here is the thing about Hymn 597, *O Day of Peace That Dimly Shines*. There is a story behind every hymn, much in the same way there is a story behind each Eucharistic Prayer. We have been using Prayer C this month, which contains the phrase, speaking to God:

At your command, all things came to be: the vast expanse of interstellar space, galaxies, suns, the planets in their courses, and this fragile earth, our island home.

Think about this. Eucharistic Prayer C was new to *The Book of Common Prayer 1979*.

What movie was released on May 25, 1977?

Star Wars.

There is strong speculation that the release of *Star Wars* influenced the language of Eucharistic Prayer C. Regardless, Episcopalians refer to Prayer C as the Star Wars Prayer.

But back to Hymn 597. The tune is *Jerusalem*, which is quite popular in the Church of England, our mother church. There was a push to include the tune in the hymnal that was being released in 1982. However, the lyrics used in the Church of England made no sense to the American Church.

In England, the tune Jerusalem supported the text of a poem written by William Blake in the early 1800s. The first stanza goes like this:

And did those feet [meaning Jesus' feet] *in ancient time,*
Walk upon England's mountains green:
And was the holy Lamb of God,
On England's pleasant pastures seen!

One interpretation of Blake's poem is that Blake imagined what England would have looked like if that nation had built an ideal society with Jesus at its foundation and not sold out to the Industrial Revolution. Blake's poem contains the phrase "dark Satanic mills," a clear reference to how the excesses of "industry" can have catastrophic effects on communities and the environment. I witnessed something similar firsthand in Michigan which was pillaged in the 1800s by the lumber industry and in the 1900s by the automotive industry.

Blake's message does not work for the Church here in the States. So, those in the Episcopal Church who wanted the tune *Jerusalem* in the 1982 Hymnal turned to composer Carl P. Daw, Jr.

The Standing Committee on Church Music charged Daw with developing a hymn using the tune *Jerusalem* and having that hymn speak to the need for world peace. We were still in the midst of the Cold War at that time.

After much prayer and struggle, it became clear to Daw that the words about peace he sought could be found in the book of the Prophet Isaiah, chapter eleven, verses six through nine, which he paraphrases in the second stanza.

Isaiah wrote:

> 6 *The wolf shall live with the lamb,*
> *the leopard shall lie down with the kid,*
> *the calf and the lion and the fatling together,*
> *and a little child shall lead them.*
> 7 *The cow and the bear shall graze,*
> *their young shall lie down together;*
> *and the lion shall eat straw like the ox.*
> 8 *The nursing child shall play over the hole of the asp,*
> *and the weaned child shall put its hand on the adder's den.*
> 9 *They will not hurt or destroy*
> *on all my holy mountain;*
> *for the earth will be full of the knowledge of the Lord*
> *as the waters cover the sea.*

***

About a month ago, we prayed the following Collect of the Day:

O God, the protector of all who trust in you, without whom nothing is strong, nothing is holy: Increase and multiply upon us your mercy; that, with you as our ruler and guide, we may so pass through things temporal, that we lose not the things eternal; through Jesus Christ our Lord, who lives and reigns with you and the Holy Spirit, one God, for ever and ever. Amen.

This Collect is rooted in the Second Letter of Paul to Timothy. It encourages us not to get so caught up in all that is wrong with the world that we lose sight of what God is doing, and that God will ultimately have the final say.

This is where the music we choose to sing in worship can help us accomplish that goal by remembering what is temporary and what is everlasting.

When we sing biblically based lyrics that speak to the challenges of our day and combine those lyrics with the beauty of music that lifts our spirits to a higher dimension, we are deep in prayer.

And, in words attributed to Saint Augustine, "... *those who sing pray twice.*"

This is the rationale for music here at St. Paul's: to sing our faith in God, to pray at a level that is both deeper and, at the same time, transcendent.

THE LETTER OF JAMES, INTRODUCTION

September 1, 2024

I invite you to turn to the Scripture insert and note the passage from the Letter of James. You may also wish to open our pew Bible to page 1272. This year there are five Sundays in September and the lectionary has assigned a passage from the *Letter of James* for each Sunday. My plan is to reflect on the Letter of James each Sunday.

First of all, who is James?

James is the half-brother of Jesus. Now, depending on your background, you might be wondering whether James was older than Jesus or younger. For those from the Catholic tradition, you might tend to think that Joseph came to his marriage with Mary widowed with children.

If you are from a more Protestant background, you will put yourself in the camp that Joseph and Mary had children of their own after Mary had given birth to Jesus.

We Episcopalians usually take the stance that it is an unsolved mystery, and it probably does not matter in the grand scheme of things.

What does matter is that James was a prominent leader of the Christian church in Jerusalem for about 20 years after Jesus had died, was raised from the dead, and ascended to heaven. So, what we have in this letter is the collected wisdom of James, how he pastored Christians during a very tumultuous time and how James encouraged his flock to live into Jesus' summary of the Law: Love God and Love Your Neighbor as yourself.

One of the things I learned while preparing for this morning is that much of what we read from James echoes what we read in Jesus' Sermon on the Mount and the *Book of Proverbs*. You will remember we had a passage a couple of weeks back from the *Book of Proverbs*, and it dealt with wisdom and how we, as followers of the God revealed in Jesus, are to walk in the way of insight. The Sermon on the Mount, of course, slaps us upside the head, waking us up to the reality that things we think are important in this life have little or no value in the Kingdom of God.

There is a word that James uses seven times in his letter, five times in the first chapter, and that word is "perfect." We see it this morning in the first sentence of verse 17: "Every generous act of giving, with every perfect gift, is from above, coming down from the Father of lights . . ."

What does James here mean by perfect? In our day, we are conditioned to believe that "perfect" means "mistake-free." Think of a pitcher in baseball who throws a perfect game: no hits, no walks, no errors. No batter gets on base. But perfect games in baseball are rare, and there are no perfect people, Jesus aside.

So, what did the concept of "perfection" mean in the time of James, and why did James encourage followers of Jesus to strive for "perfection"?

The Hebrew/Jewish understanding of a "perfect life" is not so much about not making a mistake. Striving to live a "perfect life" had more to do with living a life of wholeness, a life of integrity.

Meaning, if we say we believe in Jesus on Sunday mornings from 10:30 to 11:30, do we actually live that out Monday through Saturday, or even Sunday afternoon, for that matter?

There was a phase in my life when I was single and had no children; I certainly did not have two kids in college but there was a time when I would buy cross necklaces, crosses to put on the walls of my apartment; there was a phase when I would buy any icon I could find; many of them are on the walls in my office right now. I have acquired bumper stickers, Jesus chap-stick. Someone once gave me a Pope-on-a-Rope: it is soap on a rope, but the soap is formed in the image of Pope John Paul the Second.

I have collected a lot of religious trinkets over the years. From an outsider's perspective, I could give off the appearance of being quite the religious person. Heck, look at me now: white robe, stole, clergy shirt under these vestments.

But the point of the *Letter of James* is this: the perfect life, a life of wholeness and integrity, genuine religion, is not about the image or brand that I build for myself. None of the externals matter unless I allow God's Holy Spirit to transform me from the inside out, to shape my actions in such a way that it is clear that I have placed Jesus at the center of my life, and that my religion is not simply lip service, but that my actions confirm what it is that I say.

James cautions us not to simply hear God's word, but to put God's word into action.

I do not always succeed at this. But I am going to keep trying. And I encourage you to keep trying, as well. We can help each other.

"... *be doers of the word, and not merely hearers who deceive themselves. For if any are hearers of the word and not doers, they are like those who look at themselves in a mirror; for they look at themselves and, going away, immediately forget what they were like. But those who look into the perfect law, the law of liberty, and persevere, being not hearers who forget but doers who act-they will be blessed in their doing*" (James 1:22-25).

A PRAYER FOR THE HUMAN FAMILY

September 8, 2024

On Wednesday evening, those who attended the second session of the Alpha Course had a very honest, insightful, vulnerable, and respectful conversation about what faith in Jesus looks like in everyday life. We each expressed our joys, hopes, and struggles.

This is what we do at St. Paul's. We will not be afraid to ask the tough questions about integrating the truth of Jesus in an ever-dangerous 21st-century world, in an increasingly divisive United States of America, in a rapidly growing State of Texas, and in this rural community of Brady, Texas, that desperately needs a *Whataburger*.

On Wednesday morning, there was yet another school shooting in the United States of America, this time in Georgia. We know how this plays out in the news-entertainment media, which is quite unfortunate. Tragically, I am not sure we are as surprised and outraged as we were in 1999 with the Columbine shooting, which means we become more and more complacent when such shootings occur.

And look, I know we are impacted personally by these events. When Cade was a junior in high school in Michigan, his campus got "swatted." Swatting is where a crank caller dials 9-1-1 and tells the dispatcher that there is an active shooter, multiple people have been shot at a school, and they need assistance.

There was no shooter at Cade's high school. But, at the time, he did not know that. His teachers did not know that; we parents did not know that; and neither did the police. This happened just months after the school shooting in Uvalde. And, because of the response of law enforcement in Uvalde, a Saginaw Township police officer drove his squad car through the side doors of the school to gain entry.

Fortunately, nobody got hurt. But it could have turned out much differently.

In this morning's lesson from the *Letter of James*, the half-brother of Jesus, we read:

What good is it, my brothers and sisters, if you say you have faith but do not have works? Can faith save you? If a brother or sister is naked and lacks daily food, and one of you says to them, "Go in peace; keep warm and eat your fill," and yet you do not supply their bodily needs, what is the good of that? So faith by itself, if it has no works, is dead.

If we have faith in Jesus, regardless of how much we might honestly struggle with what "faith" means, then these words from James should cut to the core of our soul. There is nothing in here about a school shooting because the people of that day could not have even imagined what we live with now.

But the undergirding theology still holds, and we are faithful to apply it to our current situation.

If we say we care about our children, our grandchildren, or even our great-grandchildren, if we care about anybody other than ourselves, how can we stand idly by when things like this continue to happen?

Sure, we see the usual suspects on the news in the hours and days after such an event. They act on behalf of whatever special interest it is that pays their salary and, more times than not, they are calling for more restrictive laws or, on the other end of the spectrum, they will lay blame elsewhere by using vague and amorphous phrases like "mental health."

Now, you know me well enough (I think) to know that I am not a gun enthusiast, but I think you also know me well enough not to be surprised when I say that more laws on the books will not make an impacting change.

Why not?

In my humble estimation, coming up with more laws only addresses the symptoms and not the root cause.

The root cause is sin.

The human heart is in poor health because it is infected with sin; our desire to choose our own ways over God's ways.

As such, sin is the source of hate, favoritism, prejudice, bias, classism… racism: we could go on, and we will:

Last week, we heard Jesus say: "… *it is from within, from the human heart, that evil intentions come: fornication, theft, murder, adultery, avarice, wickedness, deceit, licentiousness, envy, slander, pride, folly. All these evil things come from within, and they defile a person.*"

Well, if the source of the problem is from within then the remedy for sin cannot be found within. We cannot dig deep into ourselves to find our true selves: humans cannot, on our own, "flourish" into a better, more just, and peaceful society. That line of thinking is a modern-day form of what has long been known as Gnosticism.

The solution for all that is wrong in this world comes from outside of ourselves, outside of this world, from the One who created this world, to begin with, the One who knows how things should be and invites us to live our lives as He designed.

I understand why some Christians believe the Church can bring about the Kingdom of God by influencing our politicians in Austin and Washington. Their motives are good and there is some satisfaction in seeing a bill become law. I will even admit that Christians need to advocate in the public square. Of course, there is. That is not my calling, at least not yet; but others are called to that.

However, as we engage the public square, the Church must be careful not to lose sight of its core mission.

Genuine and lasting change comes only with the transformation of the human heart.

Call me naive or idealistic, but I believe only the Holy Spirit of God can bring an end to the sin that is so easily seen in Ukraine and Russia, in Israel and Gaza (well, that entire area), in red states and blue states, and wherever we fail to recognize that people who do not think, act, or look like me are, in fact, created in the image of God and deserve to be treated as such.

When we do not see the "other" as an "image bearer of God," then we can justify in our own minds countless atrocities against the "other." We can even justify indifference, which is an atrocity on a different level.

***

In the *Book of Common Prayer*, on page 815, we have a prayer for the human family. I will close with it:

3. For the Human Family

O God, you made us in your own image and redeemed us through Jesus your Son: Look with compassion on the whole human family; take away the arrogance and hatred which infect our hearts; break down the walls that separate us; unite us in bonds of love; and work through our struggle and confusion to accomplish your purposes on earth; that, in your good time, all nations and races may serve you in harmony around your heavenly throne; through Jesus Christ our Lord. Amen.

WHAT ARE WORDS FOR?

September 15, 2024

This morning, we continue unpacking the Letter of James. We are now in the third chapter, which can be found in our Pew Bibles on page 1274. James was Jesus' half-brother and a prominent leader of the Christian Church in Jerusalem for about 20 years after Christ had been crucified, raised from the dead, and ascended to the Father.

James speaks of the need for followers of the Risen Christ to pursue wisdom and to integrate the faith into our daily lives. That is what James means when he writes about living the "perfect" life. He is not talking about being "mistake-free" it is more a case of walking the walk and not merely talking the talk.

In doing so, James draws heavily on Jesus' Sermon on the Mount as well as the Old Testament Book of Proverbs.

When I began preparing for this morning's reflection, I was tempted to write about that first sentence about not many becoming teachers of the faith. But that is not the meat of the passage. The third chapter of the *Letter of James* focuses on how we, if we claim to be followers of Jesus, use our words.

How do we allow the Holy Spirit to guide our tongues; might we add our texts and our tweets?

I remember how surprised I was when someone first pointed out to me how prominent words, language, and speech are in the Bible. I mean, it is so obvious I cannot believe I missed it. We talk about how the Bible is the Word of God and how Jesus is the Word of God, the most profound speech of God, articulated in Jesus' birth, life, teaching, death, resurrection, ascension, and eventual return.

But when we go back to the first chapter of Genesis, we read, in words, how God reveals Himself to humanity, and not just to humanity, but to all of creation. God "speaks," and creation "responds."

Words, language, and speech are important to God. This is how God communicates personally with humanity. God's commandments are given in words. God prefaces the divine commandments with the phrase: "Hear, O Israel!" God speaks; we listen. How beautiful is that? Humanity communes with God through words, language, and speech.

When God began the search for a suitable helper for "man," God formed the different animals, and the "man" spoke words to give names to each animal, somewhat paralleling how God spoke creation into existence.

Words, language, and speech are essential to our relationship with God, whether we want to build that relationship or destroy it.

Think about Genesis chapter eleven, where the people have come to the conclusion that they no longer need God and want to "make a name for themselves." One point of attack in their war was language. Verse one of Genesis 11 says: "... the whole earth had one language and the same words."

The ancient society that tried to move into the future by hijacking language could not stand before the God who uses language to be in loving communion with humanity.

Yet some people keep trying to reconstruct the tower of Babel. Some still hold to the ideology that the best way to get rid of God and have our "own way" is to control language, if not render it useless. This mindset gives birth to the idea that a word can mean whatever we want it to mean; a word can even have multiple, even contradictory, meanings.

But that claim is self-defeating.

Think about it. If I said to you "words mean nothing," that three-word sentence can only make sense if words mean something. And if words mean something, then the statement "words mean nothing" is exposed as meaningless.

It is a self-defeating attempt at a truth claim; it is false.

Words have objective meaning whether we like it or not.

If you remember the 1980s, you might recall the band "Missing Persons" and their hit, which included the following lyrics of linguistic lament by the siren Dale Bozzio:

> *What are words for*
> *When no one listens anymore*
> *What are words for*
> *When no one listens*
> *There's no use talking at all*

Of course, the song "What Are Words For" represents a cynical view of interpersonal communication with a significant other, even though it speaks the truth: words have objective meaning, but what use are words when nobody listens or, worse yet, people listen, but they disagree with what is being said?

Words, language, and speech are essential, especially when it comes to our relationship with the God we know in Jesus Christ.

If we are to live our faith "perfectly" in the sense that James uses the term "perfect," then we will choose our words wisely. We might remember from chapter one how James urges his readers to "*. . . be quick to listen, slow to speak, slow to anger; for your anger does not produce God's righteousness.*" [1]

I grew up being told by teachers that God gave us two ears and one mouth because we were supposed to listen twice as much as we were supposed to speak. I am not sure that it can be squared with Scripture, but there you have it.

The overall point is we need to be careful with our words and, in our day, our social media posts, because we need to be aware of the power of speech. The tongue is as capable of "tearing down" as it is of "building up." But I wonder if speech is used more often for insulting and belittling or playing "gotcha," going out of our way to trap people in their words.

This is what James is prompting us to think about in our own lives.

How do we speak to and about others?

How do I speak to and about people who are different than I am?

And am I considering how I speak about others who are different than I am, am I conscious that the person I am talking to is created in the image of God?

Do I choose my words wisely?

Are the words I choose consistent with the words God has chosen over the course of recorded history?

The words I choose matter because words, language, and speech are important to our relationships with both God and one another.

FOCUS

September 22, 2024

I like a good conspiracy theory. I do not believe any of them. But I enjoy the escapism now and then.

In my office, you may have noticed on one of the doors a sign labeled "Alien Crossing." It is a yellow street sign with an alien standing in front of a UFO. I got that in Roswell, New Mexico. Talk about a town that has really bought into UFOs. There is a McDonald's shaped like a UFO, there is a UFO museum, on the floor of the elevator at the hotel where we stayed, there was a picture of an alien. I mean, if you are going to go in, go all in!

On *TikTok*, I keep seeing these little videos about a pastor in Arkansas whom many believe to be Elvis Presley. According to this conspiracy theory, there are no records of this guy until 2011, which is when Elvis was supposed to have been released from the government's witness protection program. I do not think the guy looks like Elvis at all.

Lastly, I personally come up with conspiracy theories about the Church. I often wonder why the lectionary leaves out certain passages of Scripture. What do "they" not want us to read? I do not know who "they" are, and I am only joking here, but, on the serious level, I am curious why certain verses are excluded.

For example, this morning, from the Letter of James, we see that the passage omits chapter four, verses four, five, and six. So, I am always inclined to ask: what do those verses say?

Here is the answer. James writes:

Adulterers! Do you not know that friendship with the world is enmity with God? Therefore whoever wishes to be a friend of the world becomes an enemy of God. Or do you suppose that it is for nothing that the scripture says, 'God yearns jealously for the spirit that he has made to dwell in us'? But he gives all the more grace; therefore it says, 'God opposes the proud, but gives grace to the humble.'

These verses from James are about our priorities. If we claim to be followers of Jesus, does Jesus actually take priority in our lives? James consistently calls on Christians to lead lives of integrity. Know what you believe, know why you believe it, and live it!

Another section from chapter four that is left out includes verses 13 through 17, in which James writes:

Come now, you who say, 'Today or tomorrow we will go to such and such a town and spend a year there, doing business and making money.' Yet you do not even know what tomorrow will bring. What is your life? For you are a mist that appears for a little while and then vanishes. Instead you ought to say, 'If the Lord wishes, we will live and do this or that.' As it is, you boast in your arrogance; all such boasting is evil. Anyone, then, who knows the right thing to do and fails to do it, commits sin.

This is a harsh truth, and I can somewhat understand why it is omitted from the lectionary. I can make all sorts of plans for my life: what I am going to do this coming week, next year, five or ten years from now, and so on. But the reality of the matter is this: I may not wake up tomorrow morning, or something else could happen that would end my life way sooner than I expect.

Lest we believe this is a terrible thing to think about, if we claim to be followers of Jesus, then we need to be aware of how short life really is, and how it can be taken away from us in a moment. Far from being morbid, this is what helps us focus on living.

When we understand that this life is not all there is, when we understand that, because of Jesus' death and resurrection, God is preparing a place for us in eternity, then our focus on the big picture informs how we live in the moment.

This is the theology of this morning's Collect of the Day:

Grant us, Lord, not to be anxious about earthly things, but to love things heavenly; and even now, while we are placed among things that are passing away, to hold fast to those that shall endure . . .

This is a call to focus on the big picture and to understand that the decisions I make now somehow impact my eternal reality.

This is not a case of making only good decisions to get into heaven. We do not get into heaven on merit; we receive eternal life only by the grace of God in Jesus Christ.

But since we are recipients of grace, our actions in this life are to reflect how thankful we are of God's grace.

Do the decisions I make in this life communicate that I am a friend of the world? Or a friend of God?

In our nation right now, we are exerting a lot of energy when it comes to partisan politics. We are hyper-focused on election day, November 5, 2024. Far too many of us are demonizing others who do not vote the same way that "we" do, and, of course, there are some in the Church who justify their political persuasion by saying that God is on their side.

For goodness' sake, there have been two assassination attempts on a candidate this election cycle!

We all know the rhetoric employed on either side of the political spectrum is not godly.

How many millions of dollars are being spent on gaining power in Washington, D.C., instead of addressing our nation's challenges?

This is what "friendship with the world" looks like.

We want to be in power, and the end justifies the means until we get hold of the brass ring.

Like the first disciples of Jesus in this morning's gospel passage, we constantly argue about who's the greatest, and, as James says, if we deem another as being greater than we are, what sins do we commit to tear that person down to raise ourselves up?

There is friendship with the ways of the world and then there is friendship with the ways of God, seen in Jesus Christ.

What we learn in the gospel from Jesus, as well as from James, is that we in the Church – we who claim Jesus as Savior and Lord – are supposed to flip the world's script.

I believe that flipping the script begins with a single question:

What is important in life?

Where is our focus? Are we focusing only on the moment? Or are we taking seriously God's big picture, revealed in Jesus, brought closer to reality through the power of the Holy Spirit which teaches us how to BE in the moment?

Grant us, Lord, not to be anxious about earthly things, but to love things heavenly; and even now, while we are placed among things that are passing away, to hold fast to those that shall endure; through Jesus Christ our Lord, who lives and reigns with you and the Holy Spirit, one God, for ever and ever. Amen.

NACL CHRISTIANS

September 29, 2024

We have been reflecting on the Letter of James for the past several weeks. I would like to switch gears and consider this morning's Gospel passage.

I am going to all but ignore Jesus' hyperbole in Mark's gospel, the middle (somewhat) section, which calls for the amputation of body parts. We hear about things like this in publications such as the National Enquirer now and then, but Jesus is exaggerating to make a point. The problem is not with our hands, feet, or eyes, the problem is with our hearts.

Jesus calls for the transformation of our hearts. That is all we need to know about it.

Now that we have cleared that up, I prefer to spend a bit more time on the final verse from this section of Mark's gospel in which Jesus says:

For everyone will be salted with fire. Salt is good; but if salt has lost its saltiness, how can you season it? Have salt in yourselves and be at peace with one another.

We have a potluck immediately after worship, so this is as good a time as any to talk about "salt," but briefly. Like you, I am eager to see what everybody has prepared.

Consider how often "salt" is used as an image in the Bible, how salt has been used down the ages as currency (maybe the original bitcoin), for preservation, or to bring out flavor.

We can go back to the Old Testament, the book of Genesis, where Lot's wife was turned into a pillar of salt. What is going on there? The messengers of God had told Lot and his wife that they needed to flee the twin cities of Sodom and Gomorrah because God was going to rain fire on the cities for their wickedness. Lot and his wife were also told not to look back, but Lot's wife did and cue the Samantha Stevens nose twitch or the Jeannie arms-folded blink, poof, Lot's wife is turned into salt.

What does it mean to be turned into a pillar of salt? Sodom and Gomorrah are described in Genesis as "well-watered, like the garden of the Lord," near perfect ecological conditions and where there is plenty of water, there is plenty of opportunity. So the people who lived there were able to do so in abundance and luxury, and when people live in unchecked abundance and luxury, they begin to believe they no longer need God.

So-called self-reliant, self-made people start giving in to the temptation to do whatever it is they want to do and they stop listening for God. The "churchy" word for that is "sin," and sin is the reason why Sodom and Gomorrah came under God's judgment.

But because of God's friendship with Abraham, Lot's uncle, God takes measures to rescue Lot and his family from the impending judgment.

The angels tell Lot and his family to leave and not look back. But they are hesitant to do so. When we are so engrained in doing what we want, when we get out of the habit of being in relationship with God and wanting to do God's will, it is hard to turn on a dime. That is the challenge for Lot and his family.

So, when Lot's wife looks back, when she turns to look at the destruction that is being rained down on the place where she lived for so many years, the place she loved, it is because she's more interested in the "good old days that never were" instead of the new life that God had in store for her and her family. Lot's wife was preoccupied with the past. She tried to live *in* the past when she should have instead put the past behind her. There is a difference between living with the past and living in the past. Lot's wife did the latter.

That is what the Genesis story means by a "pillar of salt." Salt can be used for preservation, and Lot's wife had become consumed with trying to preserve a life that was not worth preserving.

If we have lived in any place for a considerable length of time, what do we see?

Do we see only what was?

Or can we imagine the possibilities that God has in store?

In the gospels, Jesus calls his followers the "salt of the earth." Our passage this morning from Mark alludes to this imagery which is not so much about "preservation" as it is about "flavor." Salt can bring out the flavor in food. In the same way, as followers of Jesus, we are to be salty. We are to bring out the "good" in the world. And it really does not take that much to bring out the good in others.

When I was growing up, my mother would allow me to help her in the kitchen every now and then. I do not want to say it was an everyday thing. But I did learn how to make spaghetti and even bake a few different treats.

She has this recipe for oatmeal raisin cookies, which we loved. I had seen her make them several times, and (one day) I wanted to make them on my own. So, I got out the butter, sugar, oats, raisins, and everything else it called for, including just a little bit of salt.

I was so proud when those oatmeal raisin cookies came out of the oven.

Once they cooled, my parents, brother, sister, and I started eating my oatmeal raisin cookies, and immediately spat them out.

I had messed them up. The recipe calls for one teaspoon of salt. The abbreviation for teaspoon is T-S-P. I grabbed the scooper that said T-B-S-P. I put a tablespoon of salt in a recipe that called for a teaspoon.

Don't worry. I did not bake anything for the potluck.

Jesus calls us to ". . . have salt in ourselves," but know how to proportion the salt to the main course.

I wonder if the Church sometimes mistakenly considers "salt" to be the main course, instead of simply an additive.

It is like "love bombing" where someone showers another person with so much affection, gifts, and other forms of over-the-top attention. That makes me question whether such attention is less about "love of the other" and more about control, maybe even narcissism or virtue signaling.

Some even define love bombing as "a form of psychological and emotional abuse is often disguised as excessive flattery."

Does the Church genuinely love people?

Or do we simply "love bomb" them for selfish reasons, maybe to feel good about ourselves or to make ourselves appear loving and caring and not rude or offensive?

In which case, "love bombing" is not love, certainly not the love we see from God in Jesus.

From where I stand, salt (even as Jesus uses the metaphor) is an additive, a catalyst.

The meat that God has revealed to this world is the incarnation, crucifixion, and resurrection of Jesus.

Unless our "salt" is intended for the main course that is the Gospel of Jesus Christ then, as Jesus says, our salt loses its saltiness.

"Have salt in yourselves and be at peace with one another."

RE-MEMBERING

October 6, 2024

If you look at the back of the worship bulletin, you will see many of the Bible passages I will be referencing in this sermon. You are welcome to follow along in your pew Bible, as well.

We begin with the following from Mark's gospel:

Some Pharisees came, and to test Jesus, they asked, "Is it lawful for a man to divorce his wife?"

Before we get too far down the road, I want to acknowledge how easy it is to dismiss what we think the Bible has to say about marriage. We might point to someone like King Solomon, who had 700 wives in addition to concubines, or his father, King David, who had eight wives and numerous concubines.

David even murdered (by proxy) Uriah the Hittite so he could marry Bathsheba, and yet, he is heralded as a man after God's own heart (1 Samuel 13:14).

Why would we want to look to the Bible for guidance about marriage and divorce when we see so many men from ancient cultures who were revered while engaged in relationships that subjugated and commodified women? Is the Bible misogynistic?

Let it suffice to say (for now) that just because a particular behavior is mentioned in the Bible does NOT automatically mean that God condones it. So, when it comes to topics like marriage and divorce, we need to use our brains, think critically, and dig beneath the surface.

Let's be honest:

Divorce is a fact of life. There are times when marriages simply die... and let me just say this right now: sometimes divorce is necessary, especially where there is physical and/or emotional abuse.

I have heard stories of women going to clergy for help in an abusive relationship only to have that clergyperson tell the woman to go back to their abusive husband.

That is clergy malpractice. I just want you to know I have this in mind as we move forward in the sermon.

In our gospel passage this morning, some religious leaders approach Jesus to ask him if it is lawful for a man to divorce his wife, but there is a deeper layer we do not want to miss.

What the Pharisees are really asking Jesus is: Can a man end a marriage for any reason?

This was a huge debate among people in Jesus' time springing from a passage from Deuteronomy 24.

Could men divorce their wives only in the case of "adultery?"

Or could men divorce their wives for any reason they came up with? She looked at me the wrong way; she burned my dinner; petty, sexist things like that.

Notice that the question assumes only men have agency in marriage.

The first thing Jesus does when he engages the Pharisees is to make sure everybody has their terms correct. He asks the Pharisees: What did Moses command you about marriage?

The Pharisees reply: "Moses allowed a man to write a certificate of dismissal and to divorce her."

Notice what Jesus is doing here. Jesus corrects their

misunderstanding of Scripture. The Pharisees have zeroed in on what is stated in Deuteronomy 24 while not considering the broader teaching of the Law of Moses.

Jesus informs the Pharisees that what they are using as the basis of their argument is not a "command" from Moses: it is an "exception."

There were situations where Moses allowed exceptions to the rule for pastoral reasons.

Far from being patriarchal, misogynistic, oppressive, or a so-called man of his time, Jesus challenges the notion that men should hold all the power in a marital relationship.

Jesus is counter cultural.

God's truth, revealed in Jesus, challenges and transforms the ways of the world, not the other way around.

Jesus quotes the first and second chapters of Genesis, in which we learn that God created both male and female in God's image, meaning that men and women are equal in God's eyes.

From a foundation of equality, two persons, male and female, are to join; the two become one flesh to steward God's creation in a unity that no one is to separate.

From the beginning, God's ideal for marriage, encapsulated by Jesus, is one man and one woman becoming one flesh for one lifetime.

Notice, after Jesus gives God's ideal for marriage, how we jump a bit in time here in Mark's gospel. When Jesus is alone with his disciples, the disciples ask Jesus for clarification about the marriage/divorce debate. It is only in Matthew's gospel (not Mark's or Luke's) that Jesus is recorded as saying, "... anyone who divorces his wife, except for sexual immorality, and marries another woman commits adultery." (19:12)

That takes us back to the debate from Deuteronomy 24. Jesus lands on the side of divorce being permissible in cases of infidelity... and not based on the whim of the husband.

All of this is to say:

Yes, God has an ideal for marriage we are to strive for.

That was a reality for Adam and Eve until they chose to disobey God.

Sin changed everything.

The Garden of Eden reality is something God in Christ will restore when He returns.

But until such time, we live in a broken world.

Life does not always go according to our plans.

That is why it hurts when things do not go as we think they should.

That is why we turn to our faith to learn how to cope; we draw on the pastoral care, wisdom, and grace of God we see in the Scriptures to make the best of the hand life has dealt us.

We come here to remember that where there is death, God creates new life and that God's resurrection life seldom resembles what has died (if it ever does).

Here is what I mean. Look at what happens next in this morning's gospel passage. People bring "little children" to Jesus. We might ask, whose children are these?

What if these are the children of parents who divorced?

Let's travel this road a bit.

How does Jesus relate to these children?

Jesus welcomes, embraces, and loves them. He says the Kingdom of God belongs to them.

We may not understand in our day how radical an action this is. If we think women had few rights in Jesus' day, children had fewer. It is possible that children did not have any standing in the first-century culture.

And yet, Jesus blesses these little children perhaps because life circumstances kept them from receiving the blessings they deserved or because they somehow got the impression that they were not worthy of God's blessing.

These children, all but invisible to the adults who were supposed to be in their lives, discover an abundance of God's love, grace, and healing at the epicenter of their brokenness.

There is one more thing about this passage I invite you to think about. Jesus says this:

"... whoever does not receive the kingdom of God as a little child will never enter it."

As I reflect on Jesus' statement in light of the discussion on marriage, divorce, and the pain caused by divorce and when we consider how Jesus responded to the children caught in the crossfire of human sin, I wonder: how does Jesus' posture toward the children and the posture of the children toward Jesus positively impact the parents (the adults in their lives)?

One of the things I have noticed throughout ordained ministry is that there are times when people have to make a decision (a least-worst option, if you will) they know will cause themselves and others pain and they are thrust into various degrees of despair.

They might even think they have done something so bad that it is beyond God's ability to forgive because the people they have hurt seem unwilling to forgive. At least, they are not yet at a place where they can forgive.

If you can relate to this description in any way, if you replay an event in your mind over and over and won't let it go, cannot let it go, if you have people in your life who won't let you forget it whatever it is, think of those children who were taken to Jesus when they did not feel like they had anywhere else to turn and think about how Jesus welcomed them.

In the depths of despair, Jesus relates to us in the same way he relates to the children brought to him.

In fact, we are children brought to Jesus in our brokenness.

Jesus welcomes us, embraces us, blesses us, and helps us remember that we are still, and always have been, cherished members of God's family.

Despite all the curve balls thrown our way, regardless of how we might think we have messed everything up, Jesus takes the broken pieces of our lives, re-members them (he can put them back together in a new way) for the next season of our lives. God creates new life so that we become one people, with one God, in perfect communion, not just for a moment, but for eternity.

GOD MEANT IT FOR GOOD

October 20, 2024

The Episcopal Diocese of West Texas elected a new bishop suffragan yesterday. It is Angela Cortinas, who is the associate rector of St. David's Episcopal Church in Austin. There, she works with my longtime friend Chuck Treadwell who preached here at my installation last year.

I would like to thank Michael Owens, Chris Moseley, and Mark Moseley who traveled to Corpus Christi for the electing convention. The Holy Spirit was present and active. I must tell you this is a good diocese.

I find it interesting that a bishop's election was held on the day before this morning's gospel passage in which Jesus teaches his followers what I referenced last week: that the Christian enterprise is not about upward mobility but downward mobility.

Jesus says we must be a "slave" of all, not a slave "to" all, but "of" all. We must serve people and not go around thinking that other people exist for our benefit.

Too often we look at the ordained ministry as a ladder to climb. I once held that view. But it is the exact opposite, which is why our prayer book has the following phrase in the ordination service for a bishop:

"Your joy will be to follow him who came, not to be served, but to serve and to give his life a ransom for many."

Another thing I mentioned last week was sinful humanity's penchant for violence. Specifically, we get trapped in this notion of returning violence when it is committed against us. Think of the phrase: an eye for an eye and a tooth for a tooth.

When we make that the creed by which we live, we perpetuate the cycle of violence. If someone oppresses me, then I do everything I can not to be the world's doormat. I work to get on top so that I can be the oppressor and not the oppressed. And when the people I oppressed have had enough, they mount a revolt. The cycle continues.

If I adopt a victim's mentality and can convince others that I am the ultimate victim, then I can justify all sorts of behavior, violent and otherwise, to get justice. At least, justice as I define it which probably will not be justice as God defines it.

This stands in stark contrast to what Jesus accomplished on the Cross. Jesus was victimized by humanity on the Cross, but Jesus was far from a victim even though that term is applied to Jesus quite often.

Jesus had agency. Jesus freely chose to die for our sins. Jesus did not call down an army of angels to avenge his captors. Jesus took the punishment, showing us how to end the cycle of violence.

And, as Franciscan priest Richard Rohr says, speaking of what Jesus accomplished on the Cross, if we do not allow God to transform our pain, we will transmit our pain to others.

We will perpetuate the cycle of violence.

The prophet Isaiah understood the meaning of the Cross long before Jesus was born. In this morning's gospel passage, we read these words about who was for Isaiah God's coming Messiah, and I find it interesting that this is written in the past tense:

"... it was the will of the Lord to crush him with pain. When you make

his life an offering for sin, he shall see his offspring and shall prolong his days; through him the will of the Lord shall prosper. Out of his anguish he shall see light."

That is a beautiful and profound last sentence: out of his anguish, he shall see light.

This is the result of allowing God to transform our pain, so we won't transmit it.

The book of Genesis is all about sibling rivalries: Cain and Abel, Ishmael and Isaac, Jacob and Esau, Rachel and Leah, and culminates with the story of Joseph and his ten older brothers.

Long story short, Joseph was a jerk when he was young so out of jealousy, his older brothers sold him into slavery and he ended up in Egypt, working for Pharaoh. When a famine hit, the brothers had to travel from their ancestral homeland to Egypt to get food. They had to ask their brother Joseph for help. But many years had passed, and Joseph did not look like he did when he was younger. The brothers did not recognize him.

When the brothers do find out who Joseph is, they are afraid he will retaliate against them for selling him into slavery. And Joseph, who has long since matured, settles their concerns by saying this:

What you meant for evil, God meant for good.

Ladies and gentlemen, that is the story of the Cross and Resurrection.

What humanity often means for evil, God ultimately brings about for good.

Out of anguish, there is light.

When we allow God to transform the pain that life and others inflict on us, instead of retaliation, we can make space for God's resurrection.

REFORMATION SUNDAY

October 27, 2024

Guess what day it is!

It is Reformation Sunday!

I know that is not a big deal for us Episcopalians unless you take into consideration our full-communion agreement with the Evangelical Lutheran Church in America. But this is the day that Lutherans recall how Martin Luther nailed his 95 theses to the doors of the church in Wittenberg stating his case of how the Church (Roman Catholic Church) had gotten off base. This happened on October 31, 1517.

This is why we have Lutheran hymns this morning... two written by Luther himself. You will recognize our closing hymn: *A Mighty Fortress is Our God*. You may not recognize the offertory hymn, *Lord, Keep Us Steadfast in Your Word*.

Here is something interesting I found about this hymn. You will see the first line:

> *Lord, keep us steadfast in your Word;*
> *curb those who, by deceit or sword*
> *would wrest the kingdom from your Son*
> *and bring to naught all he has done.*

This is what Luther originally wrote, at least one of the

translations from the German:

Lord, keep us steadfast in your/thy Word;
And control the murder by the Pope and Turks.

This was the prayer of Martin Luther that he put into song: control the murder by the Pope and Turks!

We know Luther had a beef with the Catholic Church. He saw where the Church was corrupt and wanted to reform it (not necessarily create a new denomination). But Luther also saw how the non-Christian cultural forces of his day worked against God's purposes, and it bothered him so much that he included the Ottoman Turks in his hymn.

I am not going to stand here and pretend like I can speak intelligently about the Ottoman Turks. I cannot; for all I know, they could be a soccer team in the German Bundesliga.

But this is the point: Luther knew that his understanding of the Gospel of Jesus Christ as justification by grace through faith had its opponents. Luther had challenges and obstacles in his day that caused him to worry about the future. But he also knew that the Gospel of Jesus Christ was worth fighting for.

Luther understood like so many other reformers did that God's Church around the world had to let go of some unnecessary practices for it to flourish in the future.

And guess what? The Gospel of Jesus Christ won out. It has been over 500 years since Luther did his thing. Yes, the Church has experienced division. We only need to drive a few blocks north on Blackburn to know that the Church still suffers from painful division.

But the Gospel of Jesus Christ endures and its continuance in Brady, Texas, is worthy of our prayer, our struggles, and our energy.

About 12 years ago, the now-late theologian Phyllis Tickle wrote

The Great Emergence: How Christianity is Changing and Why. In it, she argues that every 500 years or so, the Church needs to have a rummage sale. And what she means is this: we need to let go of what is not essential because the non-essential things hold us back from the future God has in store for us.

So, my question to you, the good people of St. Paul's, is this?

As we prayerfully consider and work toward God's future for St. Paul's in Brady, Texas, what do we need to let go of?

What is no longer essential?

We know what IS essential.

The "why" of St. Paul's or any church is the death and resurrection of Jesus Christ. We believe that the Christian worldview shows us the most accurate picture of how life is... and that the solution for all that is wrong is revealed in God becoming human in Jesus of Nazareth. We must always cling to this.

But what is not essential? What can we let go of?

Here is the thing. The best I can do is share what I am thinking now that I have been here for about 17 months. You may like my ideas or not; God may have given you better ideas and it will take me communicating my bad ideas to get you to speak up.

I am at peace with that because this is not about me.

What is about me is that I would be negligent if I failed to share with you what I see, let alone abdicating my responsibility to God as a priest in the Episcopal Diocese of West Texas.

We talked about this a little in our Saturday session on September 21, but it bears repeating.

The Presbyterian church here in Brady closed in, what, 2019?

The Christian Church closed earlier this year.

The Methodists split almost a year ago.

St. Paul's is pretty much the last of the mainline denominations in Brady along with the newly formed Grace United Methodist Church.

There are at least a couple of ways to think about this. The first way is not what I recommend. It is a thought process that says the "church" is dying and the last person to die is responsible for turning out the lights. It is an easy mindset to slip into but that level of negative, passive resignation does not interest me.

The other way to think about church trends is this: God is doing something new.

One of the things that has always caught my attention as a church nerd is the ecumenical movement, the efforts for denominations to reunite. Again, following the Reformation, Christians began to divide to keep their "church" pure. To paraphrase Dr. Phil, "How's that working out for us?"

If you find what I am about to say "offensive," I apologize in advance. But sometimes the truth hurts. The truth is that people searching for God do not care about labels like they used to.

While those inside the church sometimes turn their denominational affiliation into idolatry, people outside the church do not require a logo because a church logo, branding, or ad campaign is style and not substance.

It is cotton candy, not a rib-eye steak.

Those outside the church seek the same thing we do when we come here on Sunday mornings: the good news of God's love for all people in Jesus Christ.

So, the question becomes, how can we leverage our denominational affiliation for the sake of the Gospel of Jesus Christ?

As I mentioned, the Episcopal Church is in full communion

with the Evangelical Lutheran Church in America and we are in dialogue with the United Methodist Church, the Presbyterian Church USA, and believe it or not, the Roman Catholic Church.

If I did not know any better, I would say the Holy Spirit is planning a family reunion even if it takes another 500 years.

Given that reality what we know about the negative population trend in McCulloch County and other factors... how might St. Paul's in Brady, Texas, be thinking about, and praying for our future, for the sake of the Gospel of Jesus Christ?

God is inviting us to important work. This work will look different than what churches did ten, 20, or even 50 years ago. It will be hard. It will stretch us. It will make us uncomfortable. If you are willing to open yourselves to what God has next, you will be amazed and you will experience firsthand how God's love for all people in Jesus is worth fighting for, and sharing with, our broken world.

ALL SAINTS

November 3, 2024

We have a lot going on right now. Hopefully, we all got a bit of extra sleep last night with the time change. Maybe there is some anxiety with Tuesday being election day, although my suspicion is that most of us have voted early.

Liturgically, we commemorate with song and prayers our loved ones who have died, people we care about deeply who are now in God's direct presence. It is comforting to know that our loved ones have eternal life in Jesus Christ, but we still grieve their absence from us. The loss of a loved one hurts, no matter how long it has been since they died.

In addition, I decided to use the Bible readings from the 24th Sunday after Pentecost. These are not the readings required for All Saints; they are just part of the normal course of the lectionary. One of the reasons I have gone with these readings is the message God communicates to us in them.

Both the passages from Deuteronomy and Mark might boil down to this:

Love God. And with everything that makes us human: our emotions, motivations, intellect, and energy. Jesus says we are to love our neighbors as much as we love ourselves.

That is enough to keep us busy.

I wonder how seriously I take Jesus here, this notion of loving my neighbor as myself. There are other places in the gospels where

Jesus calls on us to love our enemies. At the foundational level, this is pretty much the same thing.

What does it mean for me to love my neighbor? To love my enemy?

What does it mean for a Republican to love a Democrat or a Democrat, a Republican?

What does it mean when we make a judgment about someone because they watch CNN, MSNBC, or Fox?

How can Aggies, Longhorns, and Red Raiders worship together at St. Paul's?

Wait. You already know how to do that!

I have heard many people say that this year's election may be the most important election of our lifetimes and that it may not be resolved on Tuesday evening after the polls close. That brings with it an increased level of anxiety.

How will we allow our personal lives to be affected by all that is going on?

How are we going to treat each other in that time of waiting?

How will we be "advent people" before the official start of the Church's liturgical season?

Please allow me to offer some perspective, wisdom from the Church. We (followers of the Risen Christ) have an important role to play right now in the life of our nation.

The Feast of All Saints reminds us that all who proclaim to be followers of the God revealed in Jesus are ultimately citizens of God's kingdom and until Christ returns and brings about the kingdom in full, we are called to be ambassadors of that realm.

Our task as Ambassadors of Christ is to announce that Jesus will return to the world and God will make things as God intends them to be. We hold fast to God's promise that He (not any government official, but He) will one day wipe every tear from our eyes and there will be no more death, no mourning, no crying, no pain.

The old order will pass away.

And when we hear Saint John use the phrase "old order," that does not mean the past four years or the past ten years. What the Revelation that John communicates here is the fallen order that was initiated when Adam and Eve first disobeyed God and brought about the sinful world into which all of us were born.

It is long past time for the mindless campaign slogans to give way to our thinking critically about the biblical narrative.

Yes, our world is broken.

Yes, we need good government to do our best in our wondrous yet imperfect humanity.

But no matter who occupies the seat behind the Resolute Desk in the Oval Office, no matter who controls the House and Senate, no matter the Governor or Mayor, our elected officials can only get us so far.

We still need a Savior.

We still need Jesus maybe even more than in recent memory.

And the world needs us to *be* the Church, the Body of Christ, in this place at this time.

Our task is to *be* the Church to help people not only see the world as God is creating it to be, but to, as we say in the Lord's Prayer, help empower God's will to be done on earth as it is in heaven.

So while we are to be engaged citizens, instead of co-opting Jesus for our personal, political benefit, we are to view what we know to be temporary with our eyes trained on the eternal, but we are to remember our resident alien/ambassador status and proclaim the message of God in Christ that comes front and center on the Feast of All Saints and All Souls, and every funeral we do, summarized in this prayer:

O God, whose days are without end, and whose mercies cannot be numbered: Make us, we pray, deeply aware of the shortness and uncertainty of human life; and let your Holy Spirit lead us in holiness and righteousness all our days; that, when we shall have served you in our generation, we may be gathered to our ancestors, having the testimony of a good conscience, in the communion of the Catholic Church, in the confidence of a certain faith, in the comfort of a religious and holy hope, in favor with you, our God, and in perfect charity with the world. All this we ask through Jesus Christ our Lord. Amen.

INVESTING IN
ST. PAUL'S

November 10, 2024

I am fascinated with our gospel passage this morning if, for no other reason than today, we begin accepting our pledge cards for the upcoming year. Now that you have had a few seconds to reflect on Jesus' words about the widow who emptied her bank account for the sake of God, let me know if you need me to print up new pledge cards so you can change your amount.

Of course, I am kidding.

There is so much more going on in this passage than how we use our personal finances to further God's kingdom on earth. For starters, Jesus has words of caution for the religious establishment. Those folks abuse their pastoral positions for personal gain and because love being popular and recognized around town, they wear fancy vestments in worship and preach for longer than 12 minutes.

We have all heard the phrase a wolf in shepherd's clothing.

The Church is not immune to abuse of power which is why clergy like me are ordained; I am "under orders," I am responsible and accountable not only to Bishop Read, the Diocese of West Texas, and the Episcopal Church but also to you and, of course, I will one day stand before God to be judged.

This is but one of the many reasons I emphasize to you that when

I teach or preach or do anything else, for that matter:

- I say my prayers.
- I study.
- I work diligently and meticulously to tell you the truth about what I learn.
- But please do not ever take my word for it.

I am not here to enable you.

I am here to empower you.

There is a difference.

I am not here to be Christian for you and to do all the Christian ministry at St. Paul's. I am here to walk alongside you and encourage you as you do the work God is calling you to do.

In the second part of this gospel passage, Jesus is watching people put money into the temple treasury. I suspect Jesus was not the only one who looked to see how much people were dropping in the collection plate. I am pretty sure the gossip trains and rumor mills were as active in Jesus' day as they are now.

A long time ago, in a parish far away, I had a parishioner come up to me proudly one Sunday after church to tell me how she had elaborately, and in a way that was obvious to others in the pew around her, placed a fake $100 bill into the offering plate.

I asked her: why did you do that?

She said: If other people see what they think is an actual $100 bill, they will put more of their own money into the offering plate.

This woman was dead serious. Deceptive. But serious. She was feeling good about what she had done until I told her she needed to start being honest about her own relationship with Jesus before she began to worry about what others were doing.

I was sorry to rain on her parade. But sometimes the truth hurts.

The Church of Jesus Christ is not a show. It is not a place to be seen for the sake of being seen nor a place to be part of the so-called "in crowd." We shouldn't come here to make ourselves look holy in the eyes of others.

We should not want to increase our attendance simply to meet our budget.

What we have to offer is the Good News of God in Jesus Christ, the God who became human, the God who walks with us in the good times and the bad and the God who died on the Cross and was raised from the dead so that we can live with Him for eternity. That is our mission, that is our reason to be: that is why we have these buildings, this beautiful campus which is a Sacrament, an outward and visible sign in Brady of God's love for all people in Jesus Christ.

Yes, it takes money to support the enterprise that is St. Paul's.

Notice that Jesus did not dissuade the people who were dropping large sums of money into the offering plate.

But the reason Jesus praised the woman who gave what the world sees as very little is because the woman invested everything she had, her entire being.

Remember the gospel passage we had last week? If we were to open our pew Bibles, we would see last week's lesson a few paragraphs above this morning's lesson: that section of Mark's gospel in which Jesus says the most important thing we can do is love God with all our heart, soul, mind, and strength and with every fiber of our being. To love your neighbor as yourself!

That is what this woman is doing!

The Christian enterprise at St. Paul's is not simply about money.

In the final analysis, every facet of St. Paul's is about you and St. Paul's is about our neighbors in Brady and all of McCulloch County.

This is a place where you can be the person God is creating you to be. to be confident in the love God has for each and every one of you in Jesus, to experience God's comfort now through His Holy Spirit and learn to love people we would not freely choose to hang out with Monday through Saturday.

St. Paul's Episcopal Church in Brady, Texas, is a place where you are invited to invest your entire being into a relationship with the God revealed in Jesus Christ, to love God with all your heart, soul, mind, and strength and to love your neighbor as much as you love yourself.

CHRIST THE KING

Reflection for November 24, 2024

Today is Christ the King Sunday and with our lesson from John's gospel, we get to eavesdrop a bit on the conversation between two different kinds of sovereigns. On the one hand, we have Pontius Pilate, who is in Jerusalem on behalf of the Roman Empire. His task is to keep the peace between the occupying Roman army and the indigenous peoples of what we now know as Israel. And by peace, what is meant here is the absence of violence, quelling the violence; think "law and order," which was likely to be accomplished best through what can only be described as "peace through strength." Governments still employ similar phrases.

Pilate was not necessarily a king; he was not on par with Caesar back in Rome; but Pilate was a man of "power."

On the other hand, we have Jesus of Nazareth who is under arrest. A careful examination of John's gospel tells us that the religious authorities convinced the Roman officials that Jesus was a threat to Caesar. But the religious elite were threatened by Jesus because Jesus had raised Lazarus from the dead, providing even more evidence that Jesus was who Jesus said he was – God in human flesh.

What do we do when we feel threatened? We are tempted to lash out and that is precisely what the religious authorities did and they triangled the government to do their dirty work for them. The religious establishment wanted the government to kill Jesus for them, which is why they claimed Jesus was a threat to Caesar, which is how Jesus ended up in Pilate's custody.

But Pilate is not stupid. He knows exactly what the religious authorities are trying to do, and Pilate is trying to clarify in his mind what Jesus means when Jesus neglects to deny the royal terminology that is applied to him.

The worst-case scenario for Pilate is that Jesus would mount an army and overthrow the Roman empire. But Jesus is clear with Pilate and others that his kingdom is not one of "power." No, the Kingdom of Jesus might better be described as one of "authority."

There is a distinction between "power" and "authority," and there is a difference in how the Kingdom of God brings about "peace."

In God's realm, "peace" is not simply an absence of war, violence, or conflict. There is so much more to peace than the absence of things that we see as negative.

More times than not, at the end of our Sunday worship, I use a blessing that is taken from Paul's letter to the Philippians (4:7) and it contains this phrase:

"... the peace of God, which surpasses all understanding, will guard your hearts and your minds in Christ Jesus."

The way I understand what our patron is talking about here is that this "peace of God" is the confidence we have in God, the faith we have in God that everything will be okay even when everything in our lives is going wrong. Or, at least, we know God will make everything okay even when life is not going how I think it should.

I do not need to tear down others for God to raise me up.

You might remember the passage assigned from the First Book of Kings two weeks ago. It is the story of the prophet Elijah, a widow, and her son. From a satellite perspective, from 30 thousand feet, that story deals with whom we trust: do we trust the God of Abraham, Isaac, and Jacob or do we put ultimate trust in things like politics, economics, self-righteousness, and whatnot?

I cannot remember for sure, but I may have alluded from this pulpit to the time when Elijah was having a pity-party. He thought he was the only one of God's prophets left and he was afraid for his life. The people to whom God wanted Elijah to speak were not doing what Elijah had told them to do, and things were not going according to Elijah's plans.

Elijah was not at peace.

So, Elijah hid himself in a cave; he went into darkness to brood. I am sure none of us has ever done anything like that. It is not a bad thing. There are certainly times in our life when we need to retreat, spend some time alone with our thoughts, and reflect. That is what Elijah was doing.

Then God repeatedly asks Elijah: why are you here?

That question works on so many levels. Why are you here? Why *are* we here?

In the middle of God's question to Elijah, God then says the following to Elijah (and this is the King James language):

Go forth, and stand upon the mount before the Lord. And, behold, the Lord passed by, and a great and strong wind rent the mountains, and brake in pieces the rocks before the Lord; but the Lord was not in the wind: and after the wind an earthquake; but the Lord was not in the earthquake: And after the earthquake a fire; but the Lord was not in the fire: and after the fire a still small voice.

This is the difference between power and authority–a sovereign who seeks to subjugate versus a sovereign who comes in love.

God was not in the wind. God was not in the earthquake. God was not in the fire.

God was present with Elijah in a still, small voice.

There have been many times in Bible study when we have wrestled with the concept of "free will" and the need to obey

God's commandments. Sometimes, we think life would be easier if God simply imposed His will on humanity. But, as we talk about repeatedly, if God did impose His will on humanity that would not be love. That would be coercion.

But God did not create us to be robots. God desires love from humanity. God created us in His image to love and for love to be love, we must freely choose to respond to God's love with love.

With God, there is no force, no manipulation. The most God can do is come alongside us, which He does in Jesus, and not berate us but speak to us appealing to our conscience in a still, small voice, a peace-filled voice.

After Elijah had heard God's still, small voice and reflected more on God's question of why are you here, Elijah was able to come out of hiding and return to his work concerned less about his own self-righteousness and more confident in God's plan for him, at peace with God and himself.

When we realize that the kingdom we so desperately need is not built through bombast by the ones with the loudest megaphones or largest armies. When it finally dawns on us that the kingdom we so desperately need comes from God's still, small voice spoken in Jesus, the Word of God, we open ourselves to that peace of God that surpasses all of our understanding, and it will guard our hearts and minds in Christ Jesus.

ADVENT 2

December 8, 2024

You may have seen earlier this week that the good people at Oxford University Press released their "word of the year" for 2024. The word, which is two words, is "brain rot."

That is right. Brain rot. Apparently, the first person to use the term "brain rot" was Henry David Thoreau in Walden, written in 1854.

However, according to the publishers of the *Oxford Dictionary*, "brain rot" usage increased 230 percent over the past year. I am not sure how they measure that, who measures it, and how much they get paid to measure word usage. But there you have it.

In this case, "brain rot" refers to what happens when we scroll the internet for hours at a time. If there is any merit to the phrase, then I have experienced an increase in personal "brain rot" since this summer, when I downloaded the *TikTok* app to my phone. I do not make any videos myself; I simply watch what other people post.

It is a scary thing. When you watch one video on *TikTok*, it somehow knows how to send you other videos like the one you watched. I mean, the technology is fascinating. It blows my mind how computers work. I mean that in a positive sense, the opposite of "brain rot."

There is one category of videos that *TikTok* keeps sending to my feed. They are videos of lawn people: landscapers. These are timelapse videos. You get to see a lot in a short amount of time.

The videos begin with an overgrown yard, and, in most cases, it is nobody's fault that the lawns got the way they did. We all know that life happens. The owners become physically unable to take care of their yards, or they pass away and these "Good Samaritans" step in.

The videos are nothing but the landscapers trimming weeds, tree branches, and bushes, mowing the lawn, bagging the grass clippings, and cleaning the driveway with power washers.

I love watching these videos.

I know. I need help.

But the reason I like these videos is because the landscapers are bringing "order" out of "chaos." At the beginning of the video, the lawn looked terrible. At the end of the video, the lawn looks great.

The videos are sacramental in the sense that the landscapers are stewarding God's good creation. The videos are symbolic of God coming into the world in Jesus to make things as they should be, and they are models of how the church should be. We are to follow God's example in Jesus and bring "order" out of "chaos."

Instead of complaining about all that is wrong in the world, the nation, the state, or Brady, instead of waiting for God passively, what would it look like to wait for God proactively? What would it be like for you and me to participate with God in making the world as God intends it?

The prophet Malachi sounds a similar refrain in this morning's Old Testament lesson. Malachi, of course, is the last book of the Old Testament. It was written maybe 430 years before the birth of Jesus.

Malachi is about how the Israelites, God's chosen people, had returned to Jerusalem after being held captive in Babylon for about 70 to 100 years. We have discussed this a bit in Sunday school.

Before the Israelites returned to Jerusalem, they had expectations about how life would be. High expectations. But their expectations were unrealistic. Life in Jerusalem was worse than what they had hoped and that is because the people were choosing their own ways over God's ways. The leadership was corrupt and instead of turning to God for help, they blamed God for all that was wrong. All they ever did was complain.

But the good news is that God remained engaged with the people even though they were not happy with God. God loved the people so much that God sent them the prophet Malachi to give them hope and to catalyze change.

With Malachi, we see a pattern:

God will send a messenger to call the people back to doing things the way things should be done and then God will show up personally to make things as they should be.

In Malachi, chapter three, God speaks through the prophet:

See, I am sending my messenger to prepare the way before me, and the Lord whom you seek will suddenly come to his temple. The messenger of the covenant in whom you delight-- indeed, he is coming, says the Lord of hosts. But who can endure the day of his coming, and who can stand when he appears?

Who is the messenger of the covenant?

If we were to skip over to chapter four of Malachi, we would see that the messenger is identified as the prophet Elijah. But how can that be, since Elijah has already been taken into heaven by a whirlwind? The "Elijah" being talked about here is "John the Baptist," the one who fulfills the ministry of Elijah. Our gospel passage this morning from Luke is about John the Baptist.

The role of John the Baptist, when fulfilling the ministry of Elijah, is clear:

For he is like a refiner's fire and like fullers' soap; he will sit as a refiner and purifier of silver, and he will purify the descendants of Levi and refine them like gold and silver, until they present offerings to the Lord in righteousness. Then the offering of Judah and Jerusalem will be pleasing to the Lord as in the days of old and as in former years.

Let's go with the imagery of fullers' soap for a moment. This was a process used in biblical times (and other times, I am sure) where a person would take a fabric and, with particular ingredients mixed with water, the fullers would dip a fabric in this solution, clean the fabric, remove whatever dirt and oil was on that cloth so that the fabric could be dyed.

This is what it means to live Advent, to heed the calls of John the Baptist to repent, literally to turn 180 degrees, to change our minds, and to live in eager expectation of Christ's return.

This is not a case of getting our acts together so that Jesus will come into our lives.

This is about bringing our lives into alignment with the God who is with us in Jesus endeavoring to live as best we can in the likeness of God or, as we see in our baptismal service, being mindful to live into the full stature of Christ so that we can participate with God as we proactively anticipate the world that God intends.

ADVENT 3

December 15, 2024

I am pretty sure I know the answer to the question I am about to ask. But I am going to ask it anyway.

Have you ever met someone who, when you first meet them or if their reputation precedes them, someone who, when you first meet them, is gruff - off-putting, defensive, or maybe even abrasive?

Margaret maintains to this day that I was rude to her when we first met, and I won't dispute that.

So, your first impression of someone is that they are rude and then you spend some time with them, have conversations with them that go beyond the weather, and realize that person is a teddy bear on the inside.

This morning, I wonder if this could be an accurate description of John the Baptist.

Here is why I think that.

John has spent many years alone living outside the big city of Jerusalem, He has no sense of acceptable fashion, and his diet looks nothing like a St. Paul's potluck.

But John has been close with God. He knows his job, he has been working toward this moment his entire life: he is the forerunner to the long-expected Messiah, Jesus. So, his task is to prepare anybody and everybody who will listen to repent, to align their lives with God, because the Kingdom of God is near.

Now, John has been traveling all around the region of the Jordan. Think Jordan River which, I am not sure how word got to the people in Jerusalem that they needed to go hear John preach. But they learned somehow, and they walked the roughly 21 miles from Jerusalem just to hear John.

If I did my research correctly, that would be like walking from here to Mason (I know it is 28 miles to Mason but stick with me). When we are done this morning, does anybody want to walk to Mason with me? I am going to pass. But you see my point: they tried to hear John the Baptist preach.

When the crowds get to the Jordan and encounter John, how does John greet them? Does he welcome them? Shake their hands? Give them a bulletin and ask them to fill out a visitor card? Or even a pledge card? Vestry nomination card?

No, John calls them a "brood of vipers." You're nothing but a bunch of snakes. What terminology do we use today? Basket of deplorables? Fascists? Socialists? Snowflakes? Aggies? Longhorns?

We use all sorts of words nowadays to dehumanize people, because (and I am speaking generally here) we think we know better than everybody else how life should be lived.

Everybody else in the world needs to adjust to whatever standard I set. You are only here for my benefit.

Please note the sarcasm in my voice. My sarcasm is thick this morning.

At the extremes, we might believe we know better than others what God wants from each of us. That is an attitude we take from time to time.

As I have read the assigned gospel passage from Luke this week, that is what I am thinking about John. Right or wrong, let's go down this rabbit trail.

Granted, for someone who lived in a desert for as long as John did, there must have been a fair amount of social awkwardness. He is meeting a large group of people for the first time in a long time and maybe that created a sense of anxiety and defensiveness within him, much like many of us experienced after the COVID lockdowns.

I get it! I am an introvert. I was socially distancing long before it was popular.

Or like any preacher, maybe John is surprised that anyone would want, let alone travel a long way, to hear what he had to say.

Whatever was in John's mind, he started off crusty and abrasive. John probably does not think that the crowds are genuine when it comes to seeking God's will in their lives. Maybe they do not care as much about God as I do. They are here only to mock me; troll me; John may have thought.

So, if I have constructed this negative idea about people whom I have never met, what should I do? I will call them a bunch of snakes.

But this is where the crowd disarms John the Baptist. They show John they are genuine, and they really want to hear what John has to say. In fact, they have been listening to his calls to repent and so, as they come forward for baptism, they ask him:

What should we do?

This is where I think John's demeanor completely changes. I imagine him standing in water up to his waist; we can hear the flowing Jordan lapping against rocks at the river's edges, and John has a perplexed look on his face: part disbelief, part joy filled.

Luke did not write it down, but it would not surprise me if John began his answer with that most eloquent of words: Uh...

This is where the fire and brimstone stops.

What should we do? The crowds ask John.

And John does not point the bony finger of shame. He is not calling the crowds snakes: he gives practical advice.

To the entire crowd, John says: if you have an abundance of clothing and food, share it. And I do not think this was John fishing for a new wardrobe and a five-star meal. He knew he could get by on what we might consider the bare minimum.

To tax collectors, people who worked for the occupying Roman empire who skimmed off the top and added fees, lining their own pockets at the expense of the most vulnerable, John says: *Don't take any more than what is owed you.*

To soldiers who, in theory, could go to just about any length to keep the peace, consistent with what he told the tax collectors, John says: Don't abuse your power.

Share your abundance.

Be satisfied with what you have.

Treat people the way you would like to be treated.

There is a fundamental question about the purpose of Advent, and I think it is the question the Church must ask itself daily.

Why do we exist? Why does the world need the Church? What is God's mission for us, the people at St. Paul's?

Our task is like that of John the Baptist, and we must learn, like John, not to be abrasive to those we might initially deem as "other."

Instead, we are to be caring when we offer practical advice and that happens only when we come face-to-face with people we might not otherwise engage.

We exist to create a safe space to wrestle with the big questions of life, to struggle with what it means for each of us to be created in God's image, and to figure out in our day, as best we can, how to live in God's likeness.

Part of that Godlikeness comes in the form of John's practical advice as we eagerly await the arrival of Christ.

John implores us to take inventory of our lives through the lens of God's bountiful grace and mercy, and respond in the following ways:

Share the abundance that God has gifted us.

Be satisfied with what God has given us.

And bearing in mind that each of us is a precious child of God, treat all of God's children the way we would like to be treated.

ADVENT 4

December 22, 2024

At the offertory, we will sing a hymn called Hail Mary, Gentle Woman. If I am being honest, because we have not heard this hymn before, it will be okay if you simply listen to it, take it in, and meditate on its words which are drawn from the same section of Luke's gospel this morning's passage is taken. This hymn comes from our Roman Catholic brothers and sisters, and I understand if some of you might be a bit skeptical of our using it in the first place.

The topic of Mary can be a contentious one for Episcopalians. However, my experience is that anxiety around Mary, the Mother of Jesus, centers more on misunderstandings about Mary and her story and that is why it is important for us at St. Paul's to not shy away from difficult conversations but to approach them with humility and an open mind.

For starters this is something we need to remind ourselves of from time to time: some people are under the impression that the doctrines of "Virginal Conception" and "Immaculate Conception" are the same. They are not.

Virginal Conception speaks to the birth of Jesus. It is the teaching of the Church that Mary became pregnant when the power of the Holy Spirit overshadowed her; Mary did not have relations with any man.

Immaculate Conception speaks to the birth of Mary. It is a relatively recent Roman Catholic dogma that states Mary was free from the stain of Original Sin when she was born.

The Roman Catholic Church also teaches that Mary did not have any children other than Jesus, that her virginity was perpetual, and that when Scripture speaks of Jesus' brothers and sisters, they were children of Joseph from his previous marriage; he may have been a widower. The Eastern Orthodox churches also follow this line of thinking.

On the protestant side of the equation, most believe that Jesus' brothers and sisters were likely born of Mary.

As Anglican/Episcopal Christians, people who try to bridge Protestantism and Catholicism, we do not require individuals to hold to a particular theology. We allow the mystery to be a mystery.

Yet all of this leaves us wondering how we, as followers of Jesus Christ in the Episcopal Church, are to relate to Mary.

What kind of help and comfort can Mary, the Mother of Jesus, offer us in the life of faith? What is it about Mary that we might emulate?

As 21st-century people in a primarily protestant, nominally Christian context, we are conditioned to dismiss what the Church has taught about Mary for two millennia. We might have an "arrogance of the present" and look down our noses at past cultures.

Like those in our day who doubt that Jesus was raised from the dead literally, some in our sex-obsessed culture doubt that Mary could have conceived the Christ child through the power of the Holy Spirit. They write off the "Virginal Conception" as hyperbole… they might even say that the Greek word for "virgin" can also be translated as "young girl" and therefore dismiss the Virginal Conception.

But these people fail to go the extra mile to understand that what the translation "young girl" really means is "not owned by a man." So, if a woman in Jesus' time was "not owned by a man" maybe even "not beholden to a man" then we are back to square one where Mary had the Christ-child through the overshadowing of the Holy Spirit.

Regardless, the story is meant to convey to us that the Savior of the world comes to us as a human being from God, not from any prestigious, powerful earthly family or nation.

As far as I am concerned, one problem with approaching Sacred Scripture from the posture of doubt or outright disbelief is that there is a hazard in failing not to trust anything we cannot wrap our minds around. Yes, we must think critically and ask questions when studying Scripture. But an agnostic or even atheistic approach to the Christian story is hubris. It places us at the center of determining fact from fiction, truth from falsehood. It removes from the equation any need to rely on God. It only serves to reduce Christianity to just another philosophy among many. I wonder if this question of "control" is behind the Episcopal Christian's potential reluctance to honor Mary, to ask the Mother of God to pray for us, not to incorporate the Anglican Rosary into our prayer lives from time to time.

But here is the thing about Mary. When approached by the angel Gabriel about bearing God and giving Christ to the world, Mary said 'yes'. Mary said 'yes' even in the face of doubters, ridicule, and even the threat of death. Mary trusted God with not only her future but her present. Mary had faith that God could create a path to salvation for her and all of humanity that she could neither see nor imagine... salvation that took on her flesh in the person of Jesus.

Mary far from being a gentle woman or quiet light was so confident in God that she could take that first step on a new journey without knowing every bend and turn on the path without worrying how God would create possibilities where humans see none.

When we travel the road of life and think we have come to a dead end, it is precisely in a moment like that when we should reflect on Mary's relationship with God. When we see no way through, when we do not know how to get from point A to point B, that is when we, like Mary, should say "yes" to God and allow Christ to be born into our lives and open ourselves to healing and wholeness.

MY CLASSMATE SANTA

Christmas Eve 2024

One of my great privileges is that I have been fortunate enough to live in many different parts of the United States of America and have become friends with so many different people.

As adults, Margaret, the kids, and I have lived in California, Michigan, and New Mexico, in addition to calling Texas home. Well, Cade did not get to live in California. We lived there in the B.C. years: Before Cade.

I was born in Virginia and grew up mostly in North Carolina but, as fate would have it, my family spent four years in Illinois, and it was in Illinois where I went to high school with Santa Claus.

Not the original Santa Claus. I am not talking about Saint Nicholas, the fourth-century bishop of Myra in what is now Turkey. My longtime friend is more of a regional ambassador of the Spirit of Christmas, one who dresses up in red suits, black boots, and deflated bishops' miters each year so that anybody who wants to can have their pictures taken with him.

He would tell you himself: he has the right physique for this job. His once youthful red hair and beard have become wintry gray over time much like the Rankin Bass Claymation version of Kris Kringle. My friend has no need for a makeup artist.

Just so you know, he is not from around here. He lives up north. Way up north. Minnesota. But, as I said, we graduated from high school in Belleville, Illinois, almost 40 years ago. We were in the band together, so we spent a lot of time with one another and other friends.

We have kept in touch over the years. Social media has been a great help with that. We have talked on the phone a couple of times and send messages probably a few times a year, often about the ups and downs of life.

We all have challenging times in life.

As wonderful as it is to come to church on Christmas Eve, every single one of us has something that weighs on our hearts and minds. So, we have come to the right place tonight.

The last time I spoke on the phone with my Santa friend, he was going through a particular set of life challenges and, if memory serves, we spoke before he accepted a role as an emissary for Father Christmas.

Once he became Santa, I noticed something different about him in his Facebook posts and the change was far from superficial.

I traded messages with him about this recently. Of course, he is always posting pictures online of him with a sleeping baby, a terrified toddler, or an embarrassed teenager.

Over the years, I have seen how his countenance has brightened.

We know how later in His life Jesus said the eye is the lamp of the body and, what I have seen in my friend might best be described with that one line from Clement Clark Moore's "Twas the Night Before Christmas":

His eyes—how they twinkled! his dimples how merry!

What I see is not mere happiness: it is joy. There is a difference. Happiness can be fleeting. Joy transcends life's circumstances.

So, I asked my friend, in addition to seeking permission to share his story, how working as Santa has made his life better, because (at some level), it clearly has.

He shared one story of a child who had it very rough early in life and was living with grandparents and they were fearful that a visit to Santa would trigger a stress response. But as it turns out, this visit to Santa was a time of healing for that child. She was able to chat with Santa about her horse; she was overjoyed at how "jolly" Santa was, and she could not stop talking about him after their visit.

And then my friend wrote this about being Santa:

"It gives me a sense that I belong somewhere and that I am good enough (which has been hard for me over the years)."

When my longtime friend embodies love, he experiences love.

On this night two thousand years ago, breaking through the darkness of a world in which each and every one of us sometimes wonder if we belong, if we are good enough, if we are loveable, an ambassador of God, an angel of the Lord, brought a message of healing to a broken world:

I am bringing you good news of great joy for all the people: to you is born this day in the city of David a Savior, who is the Messiah, the Lord.

This is the essence of Christmas.

God entered this world as a human child, vulnerable and in need of nurturing, trusting in the love of Mary, the mother of Jesus offering not momentary happiness but GREAT JOY FOR EVERY SINGLE PERSON WHO HAS EVER LIVED, regardless of circumstance.

And because the Christ Child came into the world the same way you and I did, God our Father is telling us something. God simply showing up says a lot about God, and God's presence speaks volumes about how God thinks of us.

What God is telling us on this night is something I need to hear and I suspect it is something you need to hear as well: because life circumstances often send us a different message.

What God is telling us in the birth of Jesus is this:

You belong. You are good enough. You are loved.

When God loves and when we open ourselves to experience God's love profoundly in the Christ child, God's love changes us for the better.

JESUS AND HANUKKAH

December 29, 2024

In the prologue of his gospel, Saint John writes:

"The light shines in the darkness, and the darkness did not overcome it."

Today is the First Sunday after Christmas. As is becoming my custom at this time of year (because I continue to be fascinated by and learn about this), I would like to walk us down a bit of what may seem like at first a rabbit trail. I promise to return to the main path quickly. This is one of those theological questions I like to ponder at this time of year, so I beg your indulgence.

My thinking goes like this:

- Our Jewish brothers and sisters are celebrating Hanukkah right now. It began on the night of December 25th and continues through January 2nd. It is not a fixed celebration like Christmas is for us.
- Jesus, whom we claim to be Lord and Savior, was Jewish
- So, did Jesus ever celebrate Hanukkah?

First, what is Hanukkah? Let me apologize in advance. I hope I give an accurate account.

About two centuries before the birth of Christ, the Seleucid and Ptolemaic peoples were rival empires. They were Hellenistic cultures, Greek states. When these two Greek states battled with one another, guess who got caught in the middle? The Jewish people. The land we now know as Israel/Palestine is what separated the Seleucid and Ptolemaic peoples.

So, when the Seleucids took their army through Jewish territory to attack the rival Greek state, that area naturally became Hellenized. As a result, the Jewish people were at risk of losing their identity because of what was taking place around them. Some Jewish people even adopted Greek culture, which may have been even more threatening to the Jewish way of life, the designation as God's people chosen for a specific purpose in the world.

Long story short, the Jewish people, led by the Maccabees, waged guerilla warfare against the Seleucid army because, among other things, the Greeks placed a statue of Zeus in the courtyard of the Jewish Temple, and banned Jewish people from worshiping God on the Sabbath. The penalty for doing so was death.

It took a few years, but the Maccabees succeeded in expelling the Seleucids from their land. So, they began to work on cleansing the Temple. There was concern among the Jewish people that they would not find enough purified oil to light the Menorah (the Hebrew word for lamp) which referred at that time to the seven-branched golden candelabra that was lit every day in the Tabernacle, and then the Holy Temple in Jerusalem.

But the oil they were able to use lasted not just one day but eight days, which is how long it takes to purify more oil.

Thus, Hanukkah is an eight-day Jewish holiday celebrating the rededication of the Temple in Jerusalem in the Second Century before Christ. The Hebrew word Hanukkah means "dedication."

Rabbi David Fohrman asks: why does Hanukkah draw attention to the Menorah (the light) which lasted eight days and not one?

Why not celebrate each year the Maccabees winning the war?

Well, according to Fohrman, yes, the battle that the Maccabees won solved the Jewish people's political problems at the time. Yet there were more and worse political challenges that followed and that was the case long before the current hostilities in the Middle East.

But the light on the Menorah tells a different story.

Fohrman says: God's light shined through those dark times for the Jewish people and God's light was enough, even when the people thought there was not enough of God's light to go around.

Times were "dark" because the Hellenists were trying to extinguish the Jewish people. But times were dark, too, because some of the Jewish people, according to Rabbi Frohman, were allowing the Greek culture to snuff out the Jewish culture.

It was a time, Fohrman writes, which is hinted at in the book of Leviticus. In chapter 23, God appoints festivals for the Jewish people, festivals which take place roughly between the months of what we know as March and September, months when there is more light than darkness.

When there is more light than darkness, it is easy to believe in God.

At the same time, in Leviticus 24, after God has appointed all the Jewish festivals, we read:

The Lord spoke to Moses, saying: Command the people of Israel to bring you pure oil of beaten olives for the lamp, that a light may be kept burning regularly. Aaron shall set it up in the tent of meeting, outside the curtain of the covenant, to burn from evening to morning before the Lord regularly; it shall be a statute for ever throughout your generations. He shall set up the lamps on the lampstand of pure gold before the Lord regularly.

When there is no appointed festival, when we are not in the Temple or in the Church with everybody else, when there is more darkness than light, in what, in whom do we believe?

Remember, Hanukkah did not originate in the book of Leviticus.

But there is a parallel to what we read here in chapter 24, maybe even a foreshadowing.

The question Hanukkah asks is:

Do we have enough faith in God to shine our lights in the darkness, those periods from evening to morning, those in-between spaces when we are being pulled in different directions?

Okay, so what about Jesus? What does any of this have to do with Jesus?

Well, again, Jesus was Jewish. And in John's gospel, chapter ten, verses 22-23, we read:

"At that time, the festival of the Dedication took place in Jerusalem. It was winter… (meaning it was colder than usual… a time when there was more darkness than light)… and Jesus was walking in the temple, in the portico of Solomon."

Again, the Hebrew word for Dedication is Hanukkah.

Jesus, a Jew, was in Jerusalem when the Jewish people commemorated God's light shining through the dark moments of life.

I think there is, at the very least, a theological connection between Hanukkah and the Jesus we meet in John's gospel.

Intentional or not, a truth about God emerges in Judaism and Christianity. Our tradition believes the truth reaches its fulfillment in the person of Jesus of Nazareth.

Here are the first five verses of John's gospel. This is chapter one:

In the beginning was the Word, and the Word was with God, and the Word was God. He was in the beginning with God. All things came into being through him, and without him not one thing came into being.

What has come into being in him was life, and the life was the light of all people. The light shines in the darkness, and the darkness did not overcome it.

Brothers and sisters in Christ, we experience dark times in life. That is a given. When we are enveloped in such overwhelming darkness, it is easy to think God has abandoned us and, therefore, it is logical to give ourselves over to the darkness.

But that is not what the Maccabees did.

It is not who Jesus is.

That is not what we at St. Paul's do.

In our case, you allow the light of Christ to shine through you so that others can see.

Thank you for reminding me and others that God's light shines in the darkness and the darkness cannot overcome it because, in Christ, there is enough light to go around.

ALSO BY FATHER CURT

**Making All Things New
In
Old Town**

Curtis Kemper Norman

ISBN 978-1985671379

---

[1] James 1:19